Becoming
The Woman
I Needed

A Journey Through Motherhood, Love,
and the Sacred Work of Healing

Lanya Lynn Elsa, PhD

Contents

Dedication

For Bergen,
Thank you for seeing me, for holding space for my becoming, and for reminding me that it is never too late to choose joy.

For my dad,
I feel you with me—in the quiet moments, in the signs, in the stirring of my heart. I know you're watching over me, guiding me from beyond. You've been whispering to my soul, urging me to tell my story. I wish you could hold this book in your hands, but I trust you've already seen it unfold. I miss you deeply and love you always.

Author's Note

This is my story. It reflects my memories, my emotions, and my perspective as I experienced them. Like all memoirs, it's a personal truth, not an absolute one.

I have made every effort to tell this story with honesty, but also with care. It is never my intention to cast blame or diminish the experiences of anyone who shared my life, especially Todd or our children. It is not my intent to make it sound like I did all the parenting—I just chose to speak about my own experiences and my experiences alone.

There are parts of this book that may be difficult to read for those I love. Some chapters contain raw truths about my inner struggles, my regrets, and my journey toward becoming the woman I am today. I did not include these moments to hurt, but to honor the full complexity of what it means to grow, to change, and to choose yourself, sometimes at great cost.

I will always hold gratitude for the life Todd and I built together, for the years we shared, and for the family we created. That part of my story remains sacred, even as the path we walked together came to an end.

To my sons: You are and will always be the greatest part of my life. I hope that, as you read these pages, you see not just the struggles but the deep love that shaped every decision I made.

And to anyone holding the weight of impossible choices: You are not alone.

It is never simple. It is never without risk. But it is always worth the courage it requires.

Throughout this book, I refer to Spirit, the Universe, and sometimes even past lives or soul families. I use these terms as they've shown up in my journey—each one meaningful in its own way. You don't have to believe in any or all of them to understand the truth they pointed me toward: that I was never alone, and that I was always being guided toward my authentic self.

Note to the Reader

This isn't just a story about me—it's an invitation to come home to yourself.

Throughout these pages, I share my own journey of becoming—a journey shaped by motherhood, grief, identity, healing, and rediscovering the woman I was always meant to be.

But this isn't just my story.

As you read, you may find connections to your own life between the lines—moments you've buried, questions you've avoided, dreams you've dared to revisit. That's why I've included something special at the end of this book: a companion journal filled with reflective prompts, guiding questions, and space to explore your own becoming.

There's no right way to use it. You can move through the prompts as you read each part of the book, or you can come back to them when you're ready. Whether you write one sentence or pour your heart out, this guide is here to remind you: your story matters, too.

It's not too late to choose yourself.

With love,
Lanya

Introduction

FOR MOST OF MY life, I followed the rules. The spoken rules. The unspoken rules. The invisible ones that seemed to govern the lives of women everywhere.

I worked hard to be a good daughter. A good student. A good wife. A good mother.

I believed that if I met all the expectations—married young enough, had children on time (whatever that even meant), built a beautiful home, stayed dependable and steady—I would find happiness.

And for a time, it seemed to work.

I checked every box. I built a life that looked exactly like the one I had imagined as a young woman. But even as I fulfilled the dream, something inside me was telling me that this didn't feel right.

No one tells you how isolating it can be to carry the weight of expectations, responsibilities, silence, and survival. How easily a woman can become lost inside a life that looks full from the outside but feels hollow on the inside. We're praised for our strength, our selflessness, our ability to hold it all together, yet no one asks what it's costing us. What it's burying. What it's breaking.

For years, I kept pushing forward. For my children. For my marriage. For the image of stability I had worked so hard to create. Until the day I couldn't anymore.

This book is the story of what happened when I chose myself. Not recklessly. Not without fear. And not without regret. Because the truth is, I *do* have regrets. I caused pain when I chose to leave my marriage. Real, undeniable pain. For my children. For my ex-husband. For the life we had built. But staying wasn't an option.

I was drowning. And I know I'm not alone in that feeling.

This book is about what happens when the quiet voice inside—the one you've spent years trying to silence—finally becomes too loud to ignore.

This book is about what comes next.

It's about motherhood, disability advocacy, finding yourself, spiritual awakening, heartbreak, and healing.

It's about what happens when you reach the point where you have no choice but to ask yourself:

Who am I, really, beneath all this?

And what if the life I've built is no longer the life that fits?

What if there's more? More joy. More connection. More authenticity. More peace.

My story of choosing myself may be completely different than yours. That's okay. Choosing yourself doesn't always mean leaving a marriage or starting over. Sometimes it means setting boundaries. Sometimes it means changing careers. Sometimes it simply means allowing yourself to want more—even if you're afraid.

But whatever it looks like, it's always worth the risk. You are worth it.

It's not too late. Not at forty. Not at fifty. Not ever. No matter how carefully you've built your life, it's never too late to reimagine it. No matter how long you've carried the weight of "should," it's never too late to set it down. And no matter how long you've doubted yourself, it's never too late to listen to that small, brave voice inside.

This is not a book about regrets. It's a book about becoming, not just in the practical sense, but as an awakening. A journey of remembering the parts of myself I had long silenced. It's the story of what shifted when I finally began to lay down what was never mine to carry. When I stopped outrunning the grief and instead let it sit beside me. When I released the version of me I thought I had to be and stepped into the woman I was always meant to become.

If you've ever felt the pressure to hold it all together, to be everything for everyone, to carry weight that no one else sees—this book is for you.

Come with me. Let's walk together through the unraveling...and into the becoming.

Part I

Foundations: Early Lessons on Loneliness, Desire, and Belonging

Every story begins somewhere. Mine began in the quiet spaces where I first learned to stay small, to chase approval, and to disconnect from my own voice. This section explores the early moments that shaped my sense of self, where I absorbed unspoken rules about what it meant to be good, likable, desirable, and safe. These chapters lay the foundation for everything that follows. Before I could come home to myself, I had to understand the girl who got lost trying to belong.

One

Lonely

I SIT ALONE IN my living room, cup of tea in hand, staring out a nearby window. My house is quiet, save for the soft music pouring from a speaker in the corner of the room. It's Friday night, my husband is working late, my boys are busy, and I have no plans. I don't want to go out and party; I want to stay home. I wish I had someone who would come over in sweatpants and settle down next to me with a bowl of popcorn and a bottle of wine. I wish I had someone to laugh with until my sides hurt. I wish I had someone I could talk to—I mean, really *talk to* until the sun began to peek above the horizon. But here I sit, staring at my blank phone screen with no one to call.

As I blow the steam off the surface of my tea, I watch cars pass by my house through the window, their lights momentarily illuminating my front yard. I wonder if the women inside those cars are running last-minute errands before the weekend. If they're headed somewhere fun. Or if they're rushing their kids from one activity to the next. I remember how, when my kids were in elementary school, I made connections so easily. Even so, those friendships were very specific to places and times. There was Susan, who I chatted with at pre-school pickup; Amy, who I worked with, and whose kids went to the same school as mine. Friends who I hung out with at Hunter and Dalton's private school while chaperoning field trips. Wives of our couple friends, who I noticed did so many things without me, with other wives. Those often were connections that passed the time. Real, true friendship was never that easy for me to achieve, not even when I was little.

When I was in fourth grade, I began to show interest in computer programming. There was something so comforting about a subject that had right and wrong answers with very little in between. On one crisp morning in April, I heard about a computer programming camp that was happening over our upcoming spring break. At this point, I had a sixteen-year-old babysitter named Jenny who I adored. She had bright blue eyes, braces with cool colored rubber bands on them that she had changed out every couple of weeks, and brunette hair that she wore perfectly feathered back. I remember sitting at the dining table with her while we both did our homework. I always watched her in awe, studying from textbooks that I could barely even lift. That day, I giggled and slipped the flyer over to her. "Mom and Dad said I can go! Isn't this cool?"

"Gosh, you're so rad for wanting to learn all this, Laney! Oh my God, and you'll make some friends!"

My stomach flipped at the notion—I hadn't even thought about that. But, I reasoned, it made sense. They'd all be kids I had a shared interest with. That could be an easy, natural conversation starter. I went to bed that night feeling nervous, but a little bit lighter in an odd way. For the first time, I had hope that I might meet some kids I could actually become friends with.

The very next week, Jenny picked me up in her family's station wagon with the faux wood siding. I slung my bag over my shoulder, swiped my bagged lunch from the counter and slipped into the front seat.

"Excited?" she asked, fiddling with the knob on her radio.

"Nervous," I replied.

"I get it, but I have a feeling this is going to be great!" She twisted the tuner knob once more until the static cleared and Foreigner's "Urgent" filled the car.

As soon as we pulled into the parking lot, my confidence began to wane. I walked into the building and was told by one of the camp leaders that we'd need to sit and wait for our sessions to begin. I glanced over my shoulder at a large group of kids—some my age, some older—gathered in the middle of the room. They were giggling and dancing; the girls were pretending to be cheerleaders, doing cheering as they waved imaginary pom-poms and leapt into the air. I made my way to a nearby corner and sat down, pressing my back into the wall. I sat there in awe, realizing that even if I did want to stand up and make my way into the group, I would have no idea how. They were so lighthearted and free, and that was just so foreign to me. I sat watching the girls continue to dance and cheer with tears pricking the backs of my eyes. It seemed that, somehow, with all of my introspection and striving to please others, I had forgotten to learn how to play.

Later that day, when Jenny picked me up, I got into the car and hung my head. Hot tears came quickly, cutting paths down my cheeks.

Jenny reached over and put her hand on my back. "Laney, what happened?"

"I just," I paused to sniffle, "I don't fit in."

"What do you mean you don't fit in?" Jenny reached forward and brushed my hair back with her cherry-red nails. "You're the coolest kid I know, seriously."

"You must not know many kids then," I replied.

"Listen, Laney. Tomorrow, just go in there with your head held high. Smile, introduce yourself, and just let loose. Friends will come, it just takes some effort, and that can be totally scary, but you've got this!"

I nodded, but I knew I wouldn't take her advice. It started to dawn on me that every time I'd ever "played" it was really just to meet a requirement—to make my teacher happy that I was doing something like using the blocks or clay she'd laid out for us. Little did they know that while my hands were playing, my mind was busy trying to work out the problems I perceived.

The next day at camp, I walked into the same scenario. The younger girls were dancing and running around playing tag, the boys were goofing off, and the older girls were loudly gossiping. I went to my familiar corner and sat down, looking on as the kids continued to play. That's when a buxom brunette in Calvin Klein jeans and a crop top looked over at me and narrowed her eyes. She reached out and pulled a blond girl with glossed lips close and said in a loud voice, "That creepy girl over there is just staring at us again. Why does she keep looking at us like that?"

My cheeks blanched; my heart began to race. The blond girl doubled over with laughter as the brunette pulled her away and, together, they ducked down and pretended to hide behind the group of rowdy kids. I felt so much shame, so much isolation in that moment. Moreover, I felt *heavy*. I was still a kid, so I'd never fully be able to relate to grown-ups. But even though I was a kid, I couldn't relate to other kids. I was painfully, undeniably alone.

I felt so much shame that when Jenny picked me up that day, I lied and told her that I'd made a friend. When she asked me for details, I changed the subject and cranked the volume as soon as Styx came on the radio. Jenny chatted excitedly as we drove, taking my silence as an opportunity to talk about her crush and her friends, and a big party she had gone to that past weekend—how her best friend made out with the hottest guy in school. As I listened, a lump formed in my throat. Jenny had no idea what her life looked like to me from the outside; something I knew I'd never have.

I opened my door and jumped out of the car before it came to a complete stop. I waved goodbye, then ran into my house, barely greeting my mom before I ran into my bedroom. I slammed the door and flopped down on my bed, letting the tears really come. I was finally beginning to understand that kids were cruel; they could hurt me and cause me to feel deep, pulsing shame. After several minutes of sobs and heaving breaths, I sat up and swiped the tears from my cheeks. It dawned on me that I didn't want to feel that way again; I never wanted to have my feelings hurt; I never wanted to experience such shame. And I didn't have to.

I could shut down, put up a wall, and close myself off further than I already had. I would never show weakness. I would never show emotion. I would keep those things locked up tight because if I never fully revealed myself, I never had to feel pain. I stood up and walked into the bathroom and splashed water on my face, then I walked downstairs and sat down on the couch next to my mom.

"How was it today, Sweetie?" she asked.

"It was fine," I said, picking my ragged nails.

"Good—have you made any friends?"

"Yeah," I responded. "Some."

"Is everything okay, Laney?" she asked.

"It's fine," I nodded. "I'm fine."

My mom placed her hand on my knee and squeezed. I knew that she knew I wasn't happy, but I couldn't bring myself to share with her. This pain was my own, and I had to hold it close to keep the peace at home that I so valued. In doing so, I failed to realize that I was choosing loneliness over the deep, meaningful connections I so desperately needed. I was walling myself off from Jenny, my mom, and my dad to avoid showing weakness or rocking the boat in any way. I never wanted to reveal that I wasn't perfect, because to do so, I reasoned, would make me unlovable.

Two

Learning the Wrong
Things First

WHEN I WAS IN high school, sex was this thing that seemingly
came out of nowhere. It was as if one day, everyone woke up
and decided to replace fun, innocent, imaginative play with flirting,
touching, and full-fledged making out. Gossip was rampant: who
was "going together" (dating who); who kissed who; who was having
sex and where they were doing it. It was a delicate balance—if you
abstained completely, you were a prude. If you were too sexual, you
were a slut. Walking the line was a true art form. One I wasn't quite
ready to master.

By the time I was twelve, I'd somehow managed to form an awesome
group of girlfriends. I loved spending time with them, but it wasn't
long before boys came crashing into the picture. Suddenly, my
fun, silly friends were gushing about boys, fawning over them, and
doodling their names in pink notebooks with purple pens. Although
I joined in, ignoring the boys at recess and giggling with my girlfriends

about it, this was hard on me; I still wanted to play with my dolls and watch Disney movies. I wasn't ready for all this boy stuff. Our sleepovers, once warm cocoons of movies and midnight snacks, transformed into anxiety-inducing social experiments. The first few hours were now reserved for boy-girl hangouts, turning what used to be my safest refuge into a minefield of forced interactions. While the others flirted and giggled with practiced ease, I sat frozen, unwilling to play Spin the Bottle or Seven Minutes in Heaven—okay, I played Seven Minutes in Heaven once. Spoiler alert: I almost threw up.

I managed to skirt the issue of boys for a long time, but I realized that I needed to make a change if I wanted to protect my social standing. Everyone—even the weird girl from my art class who ate paste—was hooking up with boys. I reasoned that if I didn't find someone soon, rumors would fly about me being a freak. I had to shed every ounce of "little kid" I was still clinging to and find a boy to do it with. I reasoned that if I could do it once and let people find out about it, I could finally relax and get back to doing the things I actually liked doing.

One day after school, I was fumbling with my locker when a cute, popular kid named Jeremy Swanson came up behind me. My stomach knotted itself, my heart raced, and I tried to act casual as he inched closer. He leaned forward and asked me to hang out that night. I raised an eyebrow and asked, "What do you have in mind?"

"I mean like, *hang out*. At the gravel pit?" he said, tilting his chin.

My stomach lurched—there was only one reason kids went to the gravel pit, and it wasn't to play checkers. Holy crap. It was happening. I swallowed hard, pushing my nerves aside as best I could. Jeremy was a great guy. He was smart, kind, funny, and considerate. This wasn't just a stupid date he was asking for; this was an opportunity. It was time for me to show people that I wasn't just some baby who had never kissed a boy. And I was going to prove it.

That night, after my parents went to bed, I yanked on my zipper jeans and V-neck sweater. Then, I quietly tiptoed downstairs and slid the sliding glass door open. I drew a breath and quietly made my way to the front of the house; my heart was beating so fast. I looked over my shoulder at my parents' window—their shades stayed still. I was free!

The street was silent and pitch black, save for the halogen light beaming from the streetlights that lined our sleepy street. Feeling the edges of fear creep in, I jogged the three blocks from my house to the gravel pit. As soon as I rounded the corner, I saw Jeremy standing in a beam of light cast by a nearby floodlight.

My stomach flipped as I made my way to him—he smelled overwhelmingly like Old Spice and Big League Chew. Jeremy reached out, took my hand, and began to lead the way. Together, we walked past mounds of gravel, snaking around one after another until we made our way to a dark corner, and stopped by a pile so steep, the top was pointed. I turned to face Jeremy, and before I could say anything, he wrapped his arms around my waist. He brushed the hair from my face and, trying to sound cool, he rasped, "Hey."

"Hey," I said back.

Without another word, Jeremy brought his mouth to mine. His lips suctioned around my lips; his slippery tongue made its way into my mouth. I had no idea what I was doing, but I'm pretty sure I kissed him back because soon, gravel was digging into my back and Jeremy's body was on top of mine.

I squished my eyes closed, detached, and let Jeremy do his thing. He unbuttoned my shorts and I let him wiggle them down, and before I knew it, we were having sex. Approximately fourteen seconds later, Jeremy stood up, wiping sweat from his brow. He pulled up his pants, then reached for my hand and pulled me up. I brushed at the gravel that stuck to my legs and butt as Jeremy reached into his back pocket.

Without a word, we turned and started making our way to the front of the pit, bumping shoulders now and again. When we reached the front, Jeremy looked at me in the dim glow of a nearly-burned-out streetlight, and I could tell he wanted to kiss me again.

"That was cool," he said. "We should meet up again sometime."

"Sure," I replied.

He smiled, clumsily kissed me once more, then turned and walked towards home.

Afraid of ghosts, ghouls, and serial killers, I ran the three blocks home, then quietly eased my way through the sliding glass door. My entire body felt tingly, like it was awake for the very first time. The rush was unlike anything I had ever felt; I was both satiated and starving. My entire being ached for more. It wasn't the actual sex that I loved—that part was kind of gross. It was the thing I felt right after that made me want to do it again—the delicious feeling of *significance*.

It wasn't long before everyone at school found out what had happened at the gravel pit, and soon my social status went way up. People thought

I was cool with my on-trend clothes and my group of girlfriends and the way I so casually hooked up with boys. My confidence soared; I no longer walked through the halls with my eyes down. Using sex strategically, every once in a while, became my ticket to social acceptance; all I had to do was shove my feelings down and let it happen, and I was able to reap all of the rewards without any negative consequences. The problem was that with each sexual encounter, I drifted further from my own desires; in fact, I never even knew what my desires were. Intimacy became nothing more than a quest for belonging, and I was okay with that, so I committed to using boys to get what I wanted. And it worked like a freaking charm.

Three

Experimentation

THERE ARE SOME RELATIONSHIPS you never forget. The kind that let you be unapologetically and fearlessly yourself, at last; the kind that make you feel relaxed and carefree; the kind that make you feel safe to be the most vulnerable version of you. The kind that swirl into your life and leave it a little bit different than it was before.

I had my first relationship like that when I was in my early twenties. It was with a woman named Chloe.

It started like all friendships do. We'd go shopping together, giggling and ransacking racks of clothes at the mall, checking ourselves out in changing room mirrors. We'd plan pool days where we'd lay out and exchange gossip while sipping wine coolers.

When we left her place, I was always thinking of when we would come back. Because every once in a while, when we got back to her apartment, things would take a turn. We'd tumble through the door and fall into one another, our hungry mouths meeting as clothes were peeled off. Soon, we'd be tangled in the sheets, all skin and softness, hot breath and warm hands.

Chloe and I spoke a lot, but we never had *the* conversation about what exactly we were doing. We were just friends (both actively dating men) who happened to be bi-curious; what we were doing was fun and carefree, and I have to admit, it felt really good. I'd spent all my life trying to force connections with men, especially in the bedroom. Yet, no matter how attractive I found the man or how much I liked him, sex always felt transactional. It was just what you did at the end of date two or three. It was the way you showed you were "into it." It was the way you gained significance in their eyes, and when I was young, in the eyes of others. So, I'd taught myself all the moves—the sultry stare, the low, raspy voice, and how to strategically position my body so I could just get it over with and move on.

"Being" with a woman was like an antidote to all that. It was simultaneously hard and gentle, bringing connection in place of dissociation, pleasure in place of discomfort. I had no idea what I was doing, and I liked that. I liked *her*: the way she always smelled like flowers, the way we would lock eyes and smile, even the way her voice would rise when she disagreed with me about something. We had different interests and tastes, but everything about us was easy.

Maybe, if things had been different, we could have built a future together where pool days and shopping trips were a daily occurrence. But two things got in our way: life got busy and steered us in different directions, and I had a must-do checklist that I was intent on sticking to. It looked something like this: find a suitable husband; have a white wedding; buy a beautiful house; have several children; curate the perfect life. Chloe—as much as I liked her—didn't fit into the cookie-cutter existence I'd envisioned. After we each went on with our respective lives, I stashed the memory of her in a box and secured the lid with layers of duct tape. I wasn't ready to explore what my connection with Chloe meant. That would come later—or maybe never. But I couldn't deny the way my skin remembered her fingertips, how, for the first time, intimacy felt like coming home rather than stepping onto a stage out of obligation.

Four

The Checklist

MY RELATIONSHIP WITH TODD was complicated. When we met, I was young, in the throes of building my career, throwing everything I had into curating a strong, professional reputation and climbing the corporate ladder one rung at a time. My must-do checklist remained clear—I knew I wanted to fall in love and get married. But those dreams took a backseat as I became intent on proving my abilities through meeting tight deadlines and earning promotion after promotion.

To be honest, work was the last place I expected to find my lifelong partner. My brief interactions with gruff contractors and snobbish businessmen left a lot to be desired. Sometimes I'd search the faces of the men I met on the job, wondering if they could be husband material, but then they'd make some snide remark or cringey comment that would leave a bitter taste in my mouth, and I'd instantly lose interest and move on.

Outside of work, the only place I frequented was my gym. While jogging on the treadmill, I'd see men doing sprints or lifting weights nearby. Their rippling back muscles occasionally gave me something to swoon over, but I'd shrink as I'd imagine striking up a flirty conversation. Meeting someone at the gym was such a cliché that even the possibility of it accidentally occurring made me give up on fantasizing altogether.

The timeline I had made for myself specified that I should have all my kids by the time I was thirty, and I'd recently celebrated my twenty-sixth birthday. The clock was ticking, and I was nowhere near close to achieving my goal. With anxiety churning in my guts, the constant pressure of meetings and project deadlines was a welcome distraction. I sunk myself into task after task, getting caught up in the flurry of back-and-forth emails, spreadsheets, and blueprints, trying to push down the toe-tapping, stomach-fluttering nerves that, in the grand scheme of my life, I was running woefully behind schedule.

This was particularly challenging for me to come to terms with because in every other aspect of my life, I was decidedly *on* schedule. My latest promotion had made me president of the company, and I was hitting all of my financial, health, and personal development goals. Yet, the majority of my must-do checklist—including kids and my breathtaking forever home—remained sickeningly blank. If I didn't find The One, and soon, I reasoned I would inevitably end up sad and alone with a house full of cats and no future.

It was as I entered a conference room, five minutes before a big meeting was due to start, that I locked eyes with Todd. I took a seat opposite him and opened my notebook on the table as we struck up a conversation about the project we were there to discuss. There were no lightning bolts, no immediate signs, no instant, zingy feelings of love, but after several more meetings, he asked me out for dinner and I felt a spark—it was hope.

Outside of the conference room, Todd was remarkably easy to get along with. Over artfully styled plates of sushi, our conversation flowed seamlessly. We somehow managed to avoid talking about work and instead asked one another all the usual questions and enjoyed a wandering conversation about life. As I relaxed into the comfortable pauses between bites, it struck me how incredibly down-to-earth Todd seemed. Finally, here was someone I could picture in a suit on our wedding day or assembling a crib in the nursery while I nested. I quickly assessed that Todd was everything I was hoping for in a husband and father. And he'd entered my life at just the right time.

Eager to waste as little time as possible, I allowed and encouraged our relationship to move quickly. Todd, too, seemed excited to take things to the next level, so we soon found our lives braiding themselves together. Our dates became frequent and soon they were daily, and we'd chat via phone or text in between. We moved in together in October, a mere month after we started formally dating; his family—his parents and siblings—came to visit us from California that very week; and in November, he proposed.

"I love you," he said earnestly, holding out a ring while balancing on one knee.

"I love you, too," I replied, tearing up as I accepted it.

Marry your best friend—that's the advice all couples give, right? I felt like the luckiest woman in the world because there I was, doing just that. Although our courtship was fast, Todd made me feel safe and cared for; I couldn't wish for a better friend to build a family with. Did I love him? Of course. But did I *love* him in a way that deep, soul-knowing way? I never so much as paused to consider it. I didn't even know to ask my younger self that at the time.

In the months that followed, most of our time was spent hosting engagement parties, planning our wedding from the budget to the venue, and traveling back and forth to California to see his family. Todd's mom was a kind first-grade teacher who always made me feel welcome with a gentle embrace and invitation to sit with her as she fiddled with her art projects. His dad, on the other hand, was loud and had an interesting (sometimes grating) sense of humor. The interplay between the two of them was interesting to witness; it starkly contrasted the way my parents were with one another, which I kind of loved. I watched and listened to them intently as they interacted at the dining table, assessing whether they would make good grandparents, which I knew they would. Todd also had two siblings—a younger brother and sister. Their raucous banter made me smile as I pictured my children growing up surrounded by fun, caring aunts, uncles, and cousins. I could picture my kids running around as we shared family meals, being scooped up, hugged, and loved on by these people who really felt like *home*. I loved the idea of being an in-law—being accepted into his loving family unit. The endless chatter and wedding planning kept me overwhelmingly busy. So busy that I never stopped to look within myself and ask, *Am I marrying Todd for the right reasons?*

Our wedding took place the following August, and it was everything I had dreamed of since I was a little girl. My white tulle and satin dress billowed around me like a cloud as I clutched my beautiful bouquet. My dad smiled at me with tears in his eyes as he led me down the aisle, and the room erupted in cheers when Todd and I kissed following our "I do's."

In the two months following our wedding, Todd doted on me and showered me with gifts. In the weeks leading up to our honeymoon, I'd walk in the door to find packages with my name on them, and my heart would soar. I'd tear the package open to reveal a new swimsuit or coverup, and I'd run, squealing, to embrace him. He knew just what I liked—the colors, brand, and style—and he knew that, having grown up in a household where gift-giving was synonymous with love, gifts were all I knew.

Our honeymoon passed in a blur, and just a couple of weeks later, I found out I was pregnant with our first child. Todd was the best husband I could ask for. He read every baby book attentively, attended every doctor's appointment, and cooked meals to satisfy my every craving. Every item we needed arrived in the nursery before I could so much as open my mouth to ask. I had everything I could dream of: an amazing house, an amazing husband, an amazing wardrobe, and a baby on the way. I couldn't be happier. At least, so I thought.

As I gazed into my son Conner's eyes moments after his birth, I knew I was meant to be a mom. But I was scared. Could I be the perfect parent my little boy deserved? I had no idea how to do it, but that really didn't matter. I threw myself in the deep end and loved every minute of motherhood. Conner was on my mind constantly, consuming my every waking—and even sleeping—thought. I loved him more deeply and more completely than I had ever loved anyone or anything before. And it was as I sank into this profound and fierce motherly love that my relationship with Todd began to shift.

It didn't matter what I was doing—cleaning, managing our home, or sitting across from Todd at the dinner table—I wanted to talk about our son. I soon began to notice that Todd would sigh heavily as our conversations inevitably turned towards Conner. But I didn't care. This was the phase we were in, and I was hopelessly in love. I prioritized Conner's care; I'd turn away from Todd and curl into a tight ball as I tried to get to sleep, knowing I'd have to wake several times for Conner throughout the night. And this just seemed like the *right* way to be. I didn't love having sex, so unless we were trying for our second baby, I was just too exhausted to try.

"I'd hoped our honeymoon phase would last longer," Todd said one night as I cut a kiss short to run to our crying son's bedside. I cradled Conner in my arms, breathing in his sweet infant scent, and looked up at my husband. His brow was furrowed. I wondered how our baby's adorable face didn't immediately soften him.

"We have our whole lives ahead of us," I replied. "We need to make the most of our time with him while he's still young."

I constantly wrestled with Todd's frustration. Didn't he get that kids and a family were all I'd ever wanted? I loved him. He was my best friend. I had done it. My checklist was complete. But life went how life goes—imperfectly. Neither one of us could have predicted that our little family would soon be shaken to the core. Before long, we would find ourselves barely clinging to a normal life, let alone one that was remotely ideal.

Five

The Illusion of Perfection

B EING A STAR USED to be my answer to everything. I studied hard to earn the best grades, worked overtime to get promoted, dressed with care, and planned every milestone meticulously. I had my first child at twenty-seven, just as I'd envisioned. My life was perfect and intentional. Every decision I made was meant to create a picture of success: a career I loved, a happy marriage, a beautiful home, and, above all, the family I had always dreamed of.

For the first year or so of our marriage, everything seemed to align exactly as planned. Todd and I were partners, teammates. We laughed easily. We dreamed together.

Then, when Conner was a few months old, things started to feel "off." My perfect baby boy didn't startle at loud noises. He slept too soundly. Other moms told me not to worry—"Boys are late to talk. Every child develops at their own pace!" But I couldn't shake the feeling that, with *my* son, something was wrong.

After months of referrals and testing, we finally sat in a sterile audiologist's office. I remember the smell of disinfectant, the quiet hum of the machines. The audiologist smiled gently, but her words were a thunderclap: "Your son is profoundly deaf."

I was stunned. Not just because of what the diagnosis meant, but because it shattered the illusion I had built—the belief that if I worked hard and planned well enough, everything would turn out right.

A few years later, we learned Conner had Usher syndrome, a rare condition that causes both hearing and vision loss—deafblindness. In that moment, all the usual new-parent fears—the milestones, the fevers, the sleep regressions—seemed impossibly small. My fears became vast and terrifying. Would he ever hear my voice? Would he learn to speak? How would he navigate a world built for those who can hear and see? Who would protect him when I couldn't? I didn't just fear for his future. I feared for my own abilities. Was I strong enough? Could I be the mother he needed?

From that day forward, caring for Conner became a full-time mission. We rushed from doctor to doctor. I became an expert on cochlear implants, speech therapy, orientation and mobility, educational law, and assistive technology. But expertise came with a price.

My friendships changed. I found myself withdrawing from my mom friends. Their worries—about soccer schedules, picky eating, or preschool waitlists—felt like another language. I was envious, though I would never have admitted it.

Even among other parents of children with disabilities, I felt isolated. Usher syndrome was so rare. No one else truly understood the weight of watching your child lose two senses at once.

I smiled through it. I nodded. I said all the right things. But, inside, I was terrified. And lonely.

When Cole, then Hunter, then Dalton arrived, I was determined to give each child the same unwavering dedication. Todd and I worked together as best we could. But over time, we slipped into a rhythm related to responsibilities. His job was demanding. My job was everything else.

I told myself I was fine. I told others the same. Even when friends offered to help, I rarely accepted. No one else could advocate for my boys the way I could. If I let anyone share the weight, something vital might fall through the cracks. The truth? I didn't trust anyone else to protect my children as fiercely as I could. That included Todd. Not because he didn't care. But because I couldn't relinquish control.

So I carried it all. I kept up the facade of perfection. The house stayed clean. The bills were paid. I maintained a version of my career. I volunteered. I smiled at school functions and waved from the sidelines at sports games. But the cracks began to show.

Todd and I struggled to maintain the closeness we once shared. Our conversations became logical. Our time together evaporated. My love language was quality time. His was physical touch. And between work, caregiving, and the endless responsibilities, intimacy became something I managed rather than enjoyed.

We were both trying. In our own ways. But love sometimes isn't enough when grief and exhaustion fill the spaces where joy used to live.

I told myself things would get easier. I just had to try harder, so I did. We signed up for counseling. I pushed through the exhaustion. We planned family outings, date nights, holidays, couples vacations—anything to hold us together, but I was running on empty. Even when friends and family asked how I was, my answer was always the same: I'm fine. Everything's great. But I wasn't fine. I was drowning in appointments, therapy goals, special education, and a never-ending to-do list. My greatest fear wasn't just that my children would struggle. It was that I would fail them. That I would be the reason they didn't thrive. That if I faltered—even for a moment—everything would collapse. So I kept going and, in doing so, I isolated myself even further. The weight became unbearable. The woman who once had dreams beyond motherhood and marriage became someone who measured her worth by how well she managed everyone else's needs. I longed for joy. For lightness. For connection. But I didn't know how to find it anymore.

Looking back, I can see that Todd and I were both carrying burdens we didn't know how to share. We were trying to hold together a life that no longer fit who we were becoming. It wasn't anyone's fault. It was the natural, painful consequence of years spent surviving instead of living. Eventually, the quiet question that had lingered in the back of my mind became too loud to ignore: Is this all there is?

Six

Good Girl

P ERFECT IS SOMETHING THAT'S not possible for anyone to be, yet most of us spend our lives striving for it. We want the perfect house, perfect wardrobe, perfect group of friends. But once—if—we ever secure those things, we realize that they don't equate to happiness. And then we get bored.

This was what happened to me in ninth grade. I had been the "good girl" my whole life, bending over backwards to conform to everyone's expectations of me, regardless of what I really wanted. It got to the point where I was tense with the pressure of holding the reputation I had cultivated for myself intact. So tense that I snapped.

I had finally found a friendship group that loved me fiercely and never judged or labeled me. When Mary Kate started sleeping around and even Ashley began to experiment, we held space for each other's experiences and offered our own stories and support.

Outside of school, we spent most weekends together, going on trips to a nearby shopping center with a movie theatre and bowling alley.

It was our time to forget about our responsibilities and relish in each other's company. I would link arms with Audrey or Deanne and hear about their latest boy drama. One day, when Deanne and I were alone together, I suggested, "When we go to the movies tonight, why don't we try to sneak something in?"

"Like extra candy?" she asked, nudging me.

"No, let's try to find something to drink!"

"Laney!" She widened her eyes.

"What?" I laughed. "I'm sick of being the good girl. Why shouldn't we drink in the movie theatre?"

We burst into a fit of giggles.

My parents didn't drink much, but they had a liquor cabinet with dusty bottles of vermouth and crème de menthe in it. It was the eighties, and I had a hairbrush with an end that I could unscrew to put hairspray in—I came up with the genius idea to fill it with the alcohol that I siphoned from the cabinet. Deanne and I snuck our creatively concealed alcohol out the next weekend, then bought large Cokes from Dairy Queen to pour them in, and saw a movie while completely drunk. It was the most fun I'd ever had. And we wanted to do it again.

One Saturday, after we had just swayed out of the movie theatre, Coke cups empty, we stumbled into the shopping mall. We were in fits of giggles, smelling like popcorn and stolen liquor. I was distracted, basking in the elation of being a "cool" girl who had sex and got drunk. Then, out of nowhere, we were confronted by three uniformed cops.

Our laughter stopped immediately, and despite my disorientation, I sobered up enough to return to "good girl" mode, raising my hands in a surrender and going where they ordered me to.

"What are your names?" one of them barked as he led us to a paddy wagon in the parking lot. Deanne stammered her answer. When it got to me, my voice came out like the squeak of a mouse.

As I ungracefully slid into the back of the wagon, I locked eyes with Deanne. Seeing the tears shimmer on her eyelashes was almost enough to make me burst into tears. I noticed my hands were trembling and pushed them under my legs. I avoided making eye contact with my friend for the rest of the ride.

Nauseous and terrified, the whiplash of being transported from the shiny world of acceptance and fun to the bleak reality of the dim paddy wagon caught up with me. I swallowed back bile. I wasn't a "cool" girl anymore—I was an actual "bad" girl. My heart pounded in my ears. I'd never meant for it to go this far. Was I going to jail? Had I let my parents down? Would they ever forgive me?

The cops brought us to a juvenile detention center and shuttled us into a dank holding cell with a metal toilet in the middle of it. Sobbing, we took seats on the metal benches that lined the walls, each spiraling into our own existential crisis about what would come next. Before I knew it, Deanne's parents collected her from the station. She flashed me a sympathetic look as she left me on the bench, my head in my hands. One of the officers walked over to the cell door and told me it may be a while because my parents hadn't given any indication of when they would pick me up. I stared at the scarred cement walls, numb from a mix of shock and alcohol.

I have no idea how many hours passed until my dad came to get me, but I could hear birds beginning to stir as we walked to the car. His silence on the ride home was more painful than any punishment he could give me. This was nothing compared to how I knew my mom would be when I got home. I knew I would never ever do anything like it again. Internally, I swore off drinking and having sex. I was just so ashamed. And so angry with myself.

I don't have a problem, I wanted to tell my dad. *I was just sick of being perfect!*

His silence made me hyper-aware of the lengths of my breaths and the painful lump rising in my throat. I began to cry silently. My tears stung my eyes and burned my cheeks. I tasted salt.

When we got home, my mom sat me down at the table and talked at me. I stared at my hands, at the carpet, at the cobweb in the corner—anywhere but my mom's eyes, which conveyed her extreme disappointment. I wanted to sink through the floor and make the dirt cave in on me. I wanted to sprout wings and fly through the ceiling, burst into the stratosphere and explode.

"Mom, I—" I tried to interrupt her rant, but she continued, with her firm voice. Every time I tried to interject with a defense or excuse, she spoke over me or shut me down. My throat began to close up and it felt suffocating, like I couldn't breathe, like any kind of control was out of my grasp. My mom didn't want to know my side of the story or why I'd done what I did. In that moment, it felt as though her disappointment was greater than her love for me—I couldn't think of another possible explanation.

I woke up the next day having shed my belief that to fit in, I had to do bad things and went back to the quiet, well-behaved version of myself I used to be. When Deanne waved at me from across the lunch hall, I looked away and found an empty table. I still sat next to her in Algebra, but I kept my attention focused on my work and muttered one-word answers in response to her questions.

For a long time, all of my interactions with my mom took on the same tone as the day of my arrest. I would settle down at the dinner table after an academically and socially challenging day at school just to have her talk at me instead of to me. I felt like she was saying the same things over and over and I wanted to scream. I wanted to scream that nothing she could say to me was worse than my own shame. My heart aching, I would look at my mom, her eyebrows raised, and my dad, his forehead tense, wondering, *What will it take for you to forgive me? I just want to feel loved again.*

And so the cycle continued—my belief that being loved went hand in hand with being perfect was cemented. Even now, I struggle to find anything mildly humorous in the situation. I remember the way my parents' eyes hardened as they spoke and the swirling knot that grew and grew in my stomach. But it no longer feels as world-shattering as it did at the time. Their anger faded and my humiliation went away. I can affectionately recall it as "the time I tried to be a bad girl" and accept that even though I made a mistake (as proved by the arrest), I was never unworthy of love.

Seven

Cry For Help

I SPENT YEARS WATCHING other girls swoon over their latest crushes, their eyes going dreamy as they described the way their hearts raced when that special someone walked by. But for me, those butterfly feelings everyone talked about remained as mysterious as algebra. Sure, I'd perfected the art of hooking up—treating sex like some kind of social currency that bought me belonging. But real attraction? The kind that makes your pulse skip and your stomach flip? That was a foreign concept I still just couldn't seem to crack.

By the time sophomore year rolled around, I was still doing pretty darn well for myself. I had great clothes, amazing grades, and two best friends named Lisa and Drew. They were the kind of down-to-earth, fun types who made me feel whole—we would hang out, gossip, and often talk about our biggest and wildest hopes for the future. Sometimes I'd hang out with just Drew or Lisa, or we'd all hang out together. It was exciting and fun—I felt like they brought out the best in me.

Lisa was one of the first people who I felt like I could truly be myself around. Her eyes narrowed with interest rather than disgust when I said something nerdy, and she matched my complex questions with her own. Drew was equally as open to my interests, and not only was he impossibly easy to get along with, he was also very, very good-looking. He had floppy blond hair, was always dressed in an on-trend outfit, and had the kind of smile that was contagious. Sure, he was my friend, but he also gave me butterflies when his eyes met mine, or when he playfully swatted my shoulder when he cracked a hilarious joke. I was feeling the edges of a major crush creeping in. And then, when he won the "best dressed" superlative next to me in school, I felt certain we were meant to be together.

The only problem was that I didn't actually have any experience with relationships. I'd had a decent amount of hook-ups with guys in my grade, but I'd never experienced any kind of emotional connection. I tried to look into Drew's eyes as we spoke, trying to decipher whether the attraction I felt to him was reciprocated, but all I succeeded in doing was losing track of the conversation and confusing myself even more. Unlike the uncertainty and discomfort that I usually felt with boys, being with Drew was easy. We could sit side by side at a fast-food restaurant, eating while listening to music on my cassette player in comfortable silence for hours. It was fun. It made me feel hopeful that I could soon be like everyone else and finally land a boyfriend.

My confusion about our relationship began to ease up when he and I started going out to dinner and planning times to go shopping together. I'd put a little bit of extra effort into my outfit and he'd show up looking amazing as always, and we'd head to the mall and wander around like adults. I didn't ask him, "What are we?" because it seemed obvious. We were going on dates—we were *dating*.

But then, several months into the school year, Drew slid onto the bench next to Lisa and me in the cafeteria with a huge smile on his face. He leaned in and told us we'd been invited to a party at his friend Grayson's house. His cheeks were flushed; he was so excited.

"I know it's not really your scene," Drew continued, holding up his hands, "but you should think about coming. Grayson's a really great guy, and who knows, it could be fun."

We weren't really the party types, but Drew wanted us to go and, like he'd said, there was always a small chance it would be fun. So, we agreed and started planning.

On the night of the party, Lisa came to my house so we could get ready together. We tried on several outfit combinations before deciding to match in different hues of red. We blotted cherry-colored lipstick on our lips before getting in the car and turning up the radio full volume. I drove us to the address Drew had given us. Grayson's house was abuzz—the doors were wide open, and groups of people were smoking on the front lawn. We wandered inside to be greeted by a blast of hot air and the smell of spilled beer mixed with body odor. There were a couple of people bantering back and forth, but other than that, the atmosphere had a steady hum that didn't immediately send us running.

"Where's Drew? Do you see Drew?" I asked Lisa as we shuffled past two people making out against a wall.

"He's in the other room," a guy passing by said, waving his cigarette in the direction of a closed door on the opposite wall.

I left Lisa behind to duck behind a drunk girl who was staggering towards the bathroom and turned the knob, expecting to find a huddle of boys in loud conversation. The sight I was met with made my whole body go numb. Drew was in the room alright, but he was kissing... someone else. I froze, taking in the scene. The person he was kissing wasn't just some girl from school—it was a *guy*.

"Did you find him?" I heard Lisa ask as she approached me.

I pulled the door shut and stared at her blankly for a beat before heading towards the front door. Someone bumped into me, and I barely registered their apology as I beelined for the car, my lower lip beginning to tremble. I thought we were dating. I was *sure* we were dating. But the whole time... he was *gay*?

Nobody was gay—it was 1988. The AIDS epidemic was soon to reach its peak, and kissing someone of the same gender wasn't something I had ever seen before.

My head spun. When I reached the car, I put one hand on the door and keeled over, trying to catch my breath. My eyes filled with tears as my thoughts became more and more frantic. *I'm so naïve*, I thought. *I don't understand. Why would he hurt me like this?* We were Drew and Laney; we'd both been nominated best dressed, we had meaningful conversations over dinner, our relationship was safe and real. But if that was true, then why was he kissing another boy? I let my tears fall as I grieved the perfect relationship I thought I'd finally found.

Love has a funny way of teaching its most important lessons through the relationships that don't quite work out. Drew had checked all the boxes I thought mattered—the attraction was there, he made me feel safe, and in his own way, he loved me. But as I retreated deeper into myself, afraid of the vulnerability that comes with really letting someone in, I stumbled upon a truth I hadn't expected: real connection isn't about checking boxes at all. It's about finding someone who makes you laugh until your sides hurt, someone whose soul speaks the same language as yours.

The irony is that while our romantic relationship didn't work out, Drew became something far more precious—a constant in my life, a safe harbor I could always return to. Even now, as I navigate the unfamiliar waters of understanding my sexuality, he's there, offering the kind of unconditional acceptance that only comes from deep friendship. Our failed romance taught me more about love than all my "successful" relationships combined. It showed me that sometimes the greatest love stories aren't about passion or perfect timing, but about the quiet kind of love that grows in the spaces between heartbeats, in shared laughter and understanding that transcends labels and time.

That year taught me that love isn't always what we expect it to be. Sometimes it's messy and complicated, and sometimes it transforms into something entirely different than what we initially hoped for. But if we're brave enough to learn from it, even our "failed" relationships can lead us closer to understanding who we really are and what we truly need.

Part II

Becoming—The Identities That Shaped Me

This part of the book is about the years I spent doing everything I was supposed to do—raising children, building a marriage, launching a career—while quietly drifting further from myself. I became the capable one, the advocate, the mother who always showed up. But beneath the surface, I was worn thin.

These chapters explore how that season of life showed me the parts of myself I had forgotten. The ones buried under responsibility and resilience. It wasn't a breakdown—it was a remembering. A slow, necessary unraveling that helped me see there was more to who I was than the roles I filled.

Eight

Parenting Through Grief

T HERE ARE MOMENTS IN life that split time into before and after.
For me, one of those moments came in a sterile exam room,
when a doctor looked up and said, "Your son will go blind."

It wasn't the first time our world had been rearranged by a single
sentence. Years earlier, we had already sat in another exam room and
heard the words, "Your son is profoundly deaf." That diagnosis had
upended everything we thought our life would be. And over time, we
had just begun to find our footing. We had learned how to navigate
special education systems, IEPs, and audiologists. We were adjusting,
adapting, and learning what it meant, and what it didn't mean, for our
son, for our family, for our future.

But now, here we were again. A second blow. A second unraveling.

The grief resurfaced like a roller coaster. My mind went quiet, my body
tense. I remember staring at the doctor, watching his mouth move, but

my ears felt like they were underwater. The lights too bright. My chest too tight. My breath shallow and sharp. This was my worst nightmare come true.

Todd reacted immediately. Within days, he was researching and reaching out, networking, and within weeks, we had started our non-profit, Hear See Hope, to raise money and awareness for a cure. It became our anchor—something tangible to hold onto when everything else felt like it was slipping through our fingers. We were going to do something. We were going to fix this (I now realize that there was nothing to "fix").

Years later, just when we were beginning to come to terms with this new reality, I found out I was pregnant. Dalton was born, and the joy we felt as new parents again was quickly eclipsed by that same heavy silence of another diagnosis. Another blow. We heard those same words again. Dalton, too, had Usher syndrome. It was like someone pressed rewind and forced us to relive our worst fear.

We were pulled into depression. Both of us. Quietly, inwardly. And still, we kept moving—because what else could we do?

To the world, we looked brave.

But what no one saw was the grief that we never allowed to surface.

We both dove into action. We didn't slow down. We didn't ask, how are you really? We skirted around our pain because we were terrified of what would happen if we actually let it out. We were strong for our boys. Strong for our families. And strong for each other.

But I wasn't okay. I was unraveling inside—quietly and invisibly. I didn't want to talk about it because I didn't want to see that flicker of pity in someone's eyes. I didn't want people to feel sorry for us, or for Conner or Dalton. I didn't want sadness. I wanted strength. I wanted to be the kind of mother who could handle anything. The kind of wife who didn't break.

I wish I had gone to therapy.

I wish I had let myself say out loud what my body already knew: I was grieving.Not just the diagnosis, but the life I thought we'd have. The dreams I didn't even realize I was clinging to until they disappeared.

And I wish I had told Todd how scared I was. That I didn't always want to be the strong one. That sometimes, I needed to fall apart and be held.

But instead, I became the researcher. The advocate. The one who emailed late into the night, showed up to every meeting prepared to fight, who smiled on the outside and screamed on the inside. Not because I was brave but because I didn't know what else to do with all that pain.

We were in survival mode. Living hour to hour. And in that space, our marriage started to shift—not because we didn't love each other, but because neither of us had the emotional bandwidth to fully see the other. The silence between us grew not out of indifference, but out of fear. We thought we were protecting each other by not naming the grief. But silence is its own kind of wound.

Twenty years later, when I began writing Silence and Light, I found myself reliving those early experiences with new eyes. I interviewed Todd, and we read through journal entries and notes, and for the first time, we truly shared what we had each been carrying for all those years.

That process of returning to those moments together was cathartic. Hearing Todd's version of those years—his fear, his hope, his guilt, the moments he thought he failed me, the moments he thought I didn't need him—I was stunned. I had no idea.

And then he read mine. My heartbreak. My anger. My exhaustion. My sense that no one, including him, understood the weight I was carrying. We cried. We apologized. And for the first time in years, we saw each other.

That process created what my therapist called a "shared understanding of trauma." It was messy. Emotional. But healing.

It helped us realize that trauma doesn't just come from what happened—it comes from what we never said out loud. The grief we buried to survive.

And maybe, just maybe, if we had done that work earlier—if we'd made room for each other's broken pieces—we might have found our way back sooner.

But here's the truth: we were doing the best we could.

It changed us.

That moment, that diagnosis, that grief—it didn't just alter our lives. It reshaped who we were. We both became different people in ways we couldn't yet see. In surviving, we were growing. Quietly. Separately. And for a while, we mistook that growth for strength. We didn't realize we were also growing apart.

There was a part of me that I held back—unknowingly, unintentionally. A piece of myself I protected even from him. Maybe

I was too afraid to be fully vulnerable. Maybe I didn't know how.

I don't know what I could have done differently. I've asked myself that question more times than I can count. And the truth is, I have regrets. Not about the love we shared, or the family we built, or the diagnosis, or the life we created together—but about the things left unspoken. The moments we missed. The deeper connection we didn't know how to reach for.

When I look back on my time with Todd, I do so with love. With respect. With admiration for everything he gave to me and to the boys. He showed up. He tried. We both did.

But we didn't fully see each other's fear and pain.

And because of that, we couldn't meet each other's emotional needs.

That gap—the one between what we needed and what we could offer—grew until it felt like unfulfillment. Not because we didn't love each other, but because we didn't know how to love each other through the grief. Not then.

And that is a kind of heartbreak all its own.

At times, I hurt him.

Not by intention, but through the distance I kept. The intimacy he needed, and I couldn't offer. The silence I thought would protect us, when really it was creating space between us that we didn't know how to close.

And I got hurt, too.

In all the ways someone does when their emotional needs go

unmet—not because of malice, but because neither of us had the tools, or the capacity, to name what we needed. We were both trying so hard to stay afloat, to keep the boys safe, to keep the world from falling apart around us. We didn't realize that we were losing pieces of ourselves in the process.

There is no neat ending to this chapter. Just the knowing that we did the best we could. That grief is not a failure. That silence is not strength. And that sometimes, love is not enough to carry the weight of everything unspoken.

But it was real. And it mattered.

And I will always hold it with reverence.

These experiences shaped me in ways I could have never predicted. They taught me love and compassion. They strengthened me. Taught me how to listen—truly listen—not just to others, but to myself. They helped me grow into the woman I was meant to become.

These were the life lessons I needed to learn.

And I'm a better person for having lived them.

Nine

Becoming As a Mother

WHEN PEOPLE TALK ABOUT motherhood, they often speak of the overwhelming, unconditional love that arrives the moment you hold your child for the first time. That love was very real for me. But no one tells you how quickly that love can become entwined with fear.

My fear arrived early, through small things at first: delayed milestones, missed sounds, subtle signs others told me not to worry about. But I couldn't not worry. I couldn't look away.

Eventually, the diagnoses came. First deafness. Then delayed motor skills. Then vision loss. Finally, the words that would change the course of my life and those of my children: *deafblindness*.

There was no roadmap for what lay ahead—I had to grow up instantly. There wasn't time to process or grieve or ask why. I had to become an expert on medical care, educational rights, communication methods, assistive technology, and every piece of advocacy that would give my children a fighting chance. And so I did.

Being a mother to my four boys has been the greatest teacher of my life. Through my relationships with them over the past 25 years, I've learned the delicate balance between caring for them and supporting them on their own journeys to becoming the best versions of themselves.

But before I learned how to live intentionally, I spent years running—dashing between tasks, bending over backwards to do it all. My attempts were well-meaning, but they didn't serve my family as much as I thought they did. My balancing act backfired. The relationships I had with my sons, and with myself, suffered.

When Conner was born, I was terrified. Not of pregnancy or birth, but of what would come after. How would I know what to do? Could I even be a good mother?

Once I held him, those fears softened. But they were replaced with new ones: How would I keep him safe? How would I manage the responsibilities of being his protector, his caregiver, his guide?

I embraced motherhood with everything I had. By the time he was six months old, I had mastered our routine. I balanced being a mother and a career. I kept an organized house. I checked off every task on my list.

When Conner was six months old, the words "Your son is profoundly deaf" changed everything. My carefully structured world crumbled. Suddenly, my to-do list wasn't just full—it was overflowing. Speech therapy. Occupational therapy. Doctor appointments. Research. IEP (Individualized Education Program) meetings. Navigating systems that seemed designed to overwhelm parents rather than support them.

The more challenges appeared, the harder I worked. I didn't ask for help. Even when Todd offered, I turned him away. I believed that if I couldn't manage everything on my own, I was failing. No one could take better care of my children than me.

I refused to admit how hard it was. Even to myself.

And eventually, the loneliness became crushing. Friends stopped calling. I stopped reaching out. The world narrowed until it was just my family and the overwhelming weight of responsibility.

By the time all four boys were in school, I was drowning. Every day felt like a race I could never win. Then came the moment that changed everything.

One afternoon, exhausted beyond words, I sat at my desk, buried in medical reports and IEP letters. My youngest son, Dalton, had come home from school in tears. Another son had just told me his eyesight was getting worse. The laundry was molding in the washer. The fridge was empty. My PhD reading sat untouched.

The shout from my core was undeniable: I can't do it all anymore! I feel like I'm going to crumble.

That's when I remembered a lecture from my PhD program on the concept of self-advocacy and self-determination. Until that moment, I had treated those as things I valued for my children. But I hadn't truly allowed them to practice them.

I made every decision. I controlled every detail. I thought I was empowering my sons. Instead, I was unintentionally reinforcing their dependence on me and it wasn't sustainable. That day, I promised myself things would change.

I started handing over responsibilities—slowly. First, snacks and laundry. Then, choices about clothing and participation in their IEPs. I set boundaries. I refused to do things after 8 p.m. unless it was an emergency. I learned to say "no" as often as I said "yes."

It wasn't easy. My sons resisted. They asked why they had to do things they had never done before. But over time—years—it paid off. And somewhere in that process, I realized that fostering self-advocacy and self-determination wasn't just for my children. It was for me, too.

One evening while living alone with the teenage boys, years into this slow transformation, I found myself lying in bed, glass of wine in hand, country music playing softly in the background. My to-do list still existed. There were clothes to donate, socks to pick up, emails to answer. But for once, I looked at those things and thought, I don't want to. And that's okay.

The tension in my shoulders melted. I exhaled. For the first time in a long time, I felt relaxed.

Hunter peeked inside my door and teased me, "Are you seriously sitting on your bed, drinking wine and singing?"

"Yes," I laughed. "Yes, I am."

That simple moment marked how far I had come. Breathing and enjoying my life were no longer foreign concepts. I wasn't just surviving motherhood anymore. I was becoming myself again.

Motherhood shaped me into the person I am today—not just a caregiver, but a leader, an advocate, a healer. It taught me that love is not passive. Love is action. Love is research. Love is standing up in meetings when your voice shakes. Love is setting boundaries and letting your children stumble, so they can grow. It taught me that resilience is often silent. It's forged in the private moments when no one is watching. And it taught me something else: Even the strongest protectors need protecting. Even the fiercest advocates need rest. Even the most resilient mothers deserve to be known—not just as caregivers, but as whole, complex women who carry dreams, fears, and desires of their own.

I didn't know how to ask for what I needed back then, but motherhood gave me the strength to figure it out. The same determination that once propelled me to fight for my children's futures eventually propelled me to fight for my own.

Motherhood was my first becoming—the role that shaped my purpose and demanded my strength. But as my children grew and the landscape of our lives shifted, a quiet question emerged: Who was I beyond the caregiver?

Answering that question would require a new kind of courage. A willingness to turn the resilience I had always used for others inward. A readiness to grow not just for my family, but for myself. It was the beginning of another becoming. One that would lead me to healing, to love, and to the life I once thought was out of reach.

Ten

Motherhood Made Me Brave

MOTHERHOOD CHANGED ME. BUT it didn't just shape who I was at home—it pushed me into roles I never expected to take on.

I was never the loud one.

In school, I was the girl who sat at the edge of the circle. I knew how to read a room, how to blend in, how to smile just enough. I figured out early that it was safer to be agreeable, to not take up too much space. I never raised my hand unless I was sure of the answer. I never challenged authority. I avoided conflict like it might catch fire. I just wanted to be liked. To be included. To belong.

I didn't have strong opinions—not publicly, anyway. I learned to keep the peace, to make things easier for everyone else, even if it meant staying quiet. And for a long time, I thought that was strength. I thought that was love.

But then I became a mother.

And suddenly, silence wasn't an option.

When we got Conner's diagnosis, I was still that girl—shy, unsure, terrified of getting it wrong. But I also knew I was his mom. And something primal took over. A kind of fierce, aching love that cracked me open from the inside out. He needed me. And even though I didn't know what I was doing, I knew I couldn't just sit on the sidelines anymore.

That was the moment everything changed.

At first, I didn't call it advocacy. I didn't even know that word. I just knew my son needed help, and the system didn't seem ready for him. There were so many terms I didn't understand. Why does the field of education have so many acronyms?! IEP. LRE. FAPE. There were so many professionals in the room, all speaking a language I didn't know yet. I felt like a visitor in someone else's country, trying to protect the person I loved most without a map, without a translator.

But I showed up anyway.

Even when I was trembling. Even when I second-guessed myself for days afterward. Even when I cried in the car or in the shower or quietly while folding laundry. I kept showing up. Because that's what love does.

I stayed up late learning the rules no one had taught me. I Googled terms, read books, joined online groups. I made mistakes—so many. I asked dumb questions. I apologized too much. I doubted myself constantly. But I also started learning. Little by little. Meeting by meeting. Tear by tear.

I remember one night in particular when Conner was still little, and I was preparing for another IEP meeting. I sat on the floor with a stack of papers and a highlighter, exhausted and overwhelmed. I looked over at him—he was sleeping, peaceful, beautiful—and I remember thinking: I will do whatever it takes for you. I don't care how tired I am. I don't care if I mess up. I will figure this out.

And I did.

I learned how to write emails that got answers. I learned how to push back respectfully, but firmly. I learned to hold my ground, even when professionals disagreed. Not because I wanted to fight, but because I could no longer sit by and let my child be misunderstood.

It was messy. It was emotional. And it was hard work that no one trained me for, but I kept doing it because my child needed me to.

But it was also incredibly lonely.

Most of my friends couldn't understand what we were going through. I didn't know any other moms who were navigating the same things. I didn't know anyone raising a child with either hearing or vision loss, let alone both. Before my children's diagnosis, I had never been "different." I had never been on the outside looking in. I didn't know what it felt like to be the one with the complicated forms to fill out, the awkward explanations, the invisible grief.

But once I saw the world through my children's eyes—once I witnessed how systems can fail, exclude, or ignore those who need them most—I couldn't unsee it.

Advocacy found me in the heartbreak. And it changed me.

It taught me that love shows up in unexpected ways. Sometimes it's making a hard phone call. Sometimes it's showing up to yet another meeting with a binder full of notes. Sometimes it's just refusing to give up, even when you're exhausted. Sometimes it's standing up in a room full of experts and saying, "Actually, you're wrong." Sometimes it's sobbing in the bathroom after holding it together for hours because your child didn't get what they needed—again.

But it also taught me about joy.

Because when you finally see your child supported, understood, included—when the right person walks into their life and gets it—it feels like the whole world exhales. Those moments made everything worth it.

Eventually, advocacy became more than just a response to crisis. It was the next phase of my growth. Motherhood had made me strong; advocacy asked me to be bold. It demanded that I not only show up for my children, but for myself. It became part of me. It shaped who I was. It rebuilt my confidence, piece by piece. I began to realize I had something to say. That maybe I wasn't just fighting for my kids—I was also becoming the kind of woman I had needed when I first started this journey.

So, I went back to school. Not to start a new career, but to deepen my understanding. To be able to walk into those meetings with not just heart, but knowledge. I wanted to know how the system worked so I could help fix what was broken.

And then, something unexpected happened. People started asking me to share what I knew. I started helping other families prepare for IEPs. I started writing. I started speaking. Eventually, I stood on national stages and told our story—not just for us, but for every family who's ever felt small in a meeting that should have felt collaborative.

And slowly, I stopped apologizing for my voice.

I stopped hiding my opinions.

I stopped shrinking.

Because now I see the inequities so clearly. I see how many children are left behind—not because of any lack of love or commitment from their families, but because the systems in place are confusing, exhausting, and often inaccessible. I see how often professionals forget that parents are experts too. And I know that if I stay quiet, nothing changes.

So I keep speaking.

And what surprises me most is how much joy I've found in it. Not just because I know how to navigate the system now, but because I know who I am.

Advocacy helped me become someone I never thought I could be. It pulled me further into the woman motherhood had already begun to shape. It asked more of me, but it also gave more in return. It gave me a reason to keep going when I wanted to give up. It gave me language for things I didn't have words for. It connected me to others who get it. And it reminded me that even in the darkest seasons, we can still build something beautiful together.

I'm not the same person I was before I became a mom. And I'm grateful for that. Because now, when I walk into a room, I know I belong there. Not because I have a degree. Not because I know all the laws. But because I've lived it. I've cried the tears. I've written the letters. I've shown up again and again out of love.

I never meant to be an advocate.

But I'm so glad I became one. Because at the heart of all of this—every sleepless night, every meeting, every email and phone call—are my kids. They are my greatest teachers. They are my biggest joys. Their strength, their humor, their resilience—it's what keeps me going. Watching them grow into who they are has been the most beautiful part of this journey. Like when Conner shared his story in front of a room full of adults, calm and confident, showing a wisdom beyond his years. Or when Dalton asked to be part of an IEP meeting so he could advocate for the accommodations he knew he needed. These moments stop me in my tracks—they remind me that everything we've fought for is becoming part of who they are. They are the reason I found my voice, and the reason I'll never stop using it. And now, I get to watch them find their own voices. I see them becoming advocates in their own ways—strong, thoughtful, and unafraid to speak up. I'm so proud of who they are and who they're becoming.

And here's what I know now: the girl I used to be—the one who stayed quiet to keep the peace—didn't disappear. She grew. She didn't become fearless, but she became willing. Advocacy didn't change who I was—it peeled back the layers I had built to stay small. It forced me to face parts of myself I might have avoided otherwise.

And while I've found strength and clarity in the process, it hasn't made everything easier. I still walk into meetings with knots in my stomach. I still get tired. I still grieve. There are days when I want to hand it all off and just be a mom again, without the weight of constant responsibility or the pressure to always be the one holding it all together.

But I keep showing up—because my kids are watching. And because families like ours deserve better. We deserve to be seen, to be heard, and to have our stories matter. Love made me brave. And it still does.

That's what advocacy has become for me. Not a role I chose, but one I've grown into. Not because it's easy, but because it's necessary. And even though the road has been long and often lonely, I wouldn't take a different path. Every time I use my voice, I feel more grounded in who I am. Advocacy has given me not just a purpose, but a deeper sense of connection—to my children, to other families, and to the quiet girl I used to be. She didn't disappear. She just learned to speak.

Eleven

To Be Liked

ALL I WANTED WAS for everyone to like me—for them to smile when I spoke, say nice things when I wasn't in the room, and maybe even admire me, just a little. The idea of being the person who caused discomfort or made other people's lives harder struck me with terror. I wanted to be the kind of person who made everyone feel good, all the time. At the root of it all, I really just wanted to belong, and being liked seemed to be the key to belonging.

As I went through elementary school, I became adept at reading people's expressions. Dimples were a good thing and a sharp line between a person's eyebrows was bad. When I noticed signs of upset creeping into someone's eyes, I would pause, evaluate what caused it, and change my actions to make the situation better. The problem was that although I learned how to avoid upsetting people, I couldn't seem to take things any further. No matter how badly I wanted to, I couldn't seem to turn them into friends.

It was easy enough to stack blocks next to them and show them how to color within the lines, but outside of the classroom, I didn't know how to act. I would sit on the metal bench on the playground and stare at my classmates running around and laughing together in such a carefree way. I fidgeted with my hands. Why couldn't I do that?

Whenever someone waved me over and asked me to join in, I spent the entire game following along with effort and precision, my shoulders tense with the concern that I would accidentally break the rules or somehow ruin the game for everyone else. The idea that playing was supposed to be fun was a foreign concept to me. It was a heavy activity. How did others make it seem so... light?

As time progressed, the space between me and my peers widened into a chasm. Almost everything they did was incomprehensible: the amount of noise they made when our teacher was trying to talk, the long list of excuses for why they couldn't do their homework, their childish jokes, and their random boy band obsessions. As I grew more and more perplexed by their behavior, I found myself empathizing with my teachers. I saw how much it overwhelmed them when everyone spoke at once and how sad they were when no one wanted to pay attention to their lessons.

It was hard being a kid, yet relating so much more easily to adults. While I could form connections with my teachers, they were limited to the usual adult-child dynamic. I felt as if I existed in a sort of limbo—a reality somewhere between adulthood and childhood. My whole body ached to belong to one or the other, but mentally I was hopelessly trapped in between. Staring into space during classes became my norm. I would daydream about what it would be like to have friends who

I understood and who understood me. What would we talk about during lunch? What kind of games would we play? I liked controlling all the characters in my daydreams—I knew what they were about to say or do before they did it. I could anticipate everything, from the actions to the emotions. Real life would be so much easier if it played out like that.

As it was, I spent every conversation trying to process social cues that others read naturally. But no one knew just how much I was torturing myself. I spent my days performing the role of someone who had it all together—nodding at the right moments, smiling when expected, pretending I wasn't constantly scanning every room for signs of rejection. But inside, my anxiety hummed like a live wire, ready to spark at the slightest hint of discomfort. All I wanted was just one friendship where I could let that mask slip, where I didn't have to calculate every word and gesture. The kind of easy connection that other people seemed to form without trying. But after years of keeping everyone at arm's length, I had no idea how to even begin.

I was still maintaining this façade. I sat in a restaurant surrounded by friends, suppressing the feeling that I wanted to be anywhere else. While Todd gestured wildly beside me, recounting a story I'd heard several times before, I shoved salad into my mouth and tried not to spill any on my dress. I was the only one at the table without a glass of wine. It had seemed like a smart decision when I'd ordered (alcohol just made me tired, then unable to sleep) but now I wished I had something to help me get through the evening.

Strangers turned to look at our table as Todd finished his story and everyone burst into unrestrained, boisterous laughter. I forced a laugh, too, feeling my cheeks burn. Didn't they know they were disturbing everyone else in the restaurant?

"How are you doing, Lane?" one of the women asked, reaching across the table to touch my hand.

"Oh, I'm fine," I replied, mustering a smile. I didn't know how I was actually doing, but I wasn't about to confess that—what would she even do if I did? "Fine" was the acceptable response. The safe one.

"We heard about Dalton's diagnosis," she continued.

"Yeah, it sucks," I replied. "But, you know, we're just going day by day—"

A server stopped at our table to clear our empty plates, and the men began to talk amongst themselves. I folded my hands in my lap, partly relieved that I'd been spared the need to explain further and partly frustrated that such a minor interaction was the extent of my so-called friends' support.

I sipped my Diet Coke and zoned out again. They didn't really care about me. They didn't even see the real me. They saw a woman with a nice house, a husband, a job, and four sons. Even though my kids had disabilities, my life was still too perfect to pity.

I half-heartedly tried to engage with the women's conversation, which had turned to gossip about someone's neighbor. They were supposed to be my best friends, but I was feeling like I had in elementary school—like a chasm had opened up between us. How could they sit there and complain about their day when the world was so vast and complex?

After several minutes of trying and failing to concentrate, I turned my body towards the men. Their discussion about business was instantly easier for me to participate in. I knew that world—I had been part of it since my last semester of college. Sharing my thoughts and asking questions about it came naturally; chatting with the men, I was finally enjoying myself. But then, I heard a laugh from one of the women, and she said, "What's Lane doing over there?"

"Yeah, are you stealing our husbands, Lane?"

I chuckled awkwardly. Right, I'd forgotten. I wasn't doing what I was supposed to. Being a woman and a wife came before being a businessperson.

Todd's hand found my arm as he turned to them. "My wife is so smart," he announced to the table. "She's getting her PhD, she's killing it at work, and she takes care of our kids. I am so proud of her."

Awws and oohs arose from the group, and I began to smile, appreciative that he'd stood up for me.

"She really knows what she's doing with her life," Todd continued. "You're so lucky to have that, you know?" he said to me with everyone still listening. "You're really helping people, and all I'm doing is building houses!"

Everyone laughed again and I tried to join in, but I could feel something different behind his words. *You're happy*, he was saying, *and I'm not!*

Not one person in the group asked me how my dissertation was going.

Just pretend you're a stupid woman who doesn't know anything and doesn't matter, it felt like they were saying. I took another gulp of my Diet Coke.

"What is it you do for work, Lane?" one woman asked.

"Ah." I looked over at her, trying to hide my sudden nausea. "I work in advocacy," I said quietly.

"That's so awesome. What does it involve?"

I stared at her for a moment, conscious of Todd next to me. "It's—um... I don't know," I muttered, at a loss for words. How could I explain it without getting into business details that the women didn't want to hear or without talking about how I was helping people and upsetting Todd? "It's complicated, I guess. Do you work?"

The conversation continued without me, and I breathed a sigh of relief. I overheard the men start a discussion about politics—something about social services—and thought about all of the opinions I would have to offer if I had been included. As it was, I wasn't welcome, so I kept my mouth shut.

As Todd turned the key in the car after dinner, I stared out the window, my head spinning. I'd spent the entire dinner self-censoring—being someone other than myself. And, why? I cared so much about what those people thought about me, but they didn't even care enough to dig for a genuine answer to, "How are you?" I let out a shaky breath as Todd recounted a conversation I'd missed when I was talking to the women.

I had succeeded in my mission of being liked, yet I was further than ever from feeling like I belonged. It dawned on me that I would never find acceptance, connection, and belonging as long as I was pretending to be someone else. I didn't want to be liked for being someone others wanted me to be. I wanted to be loved for who I was.

Twelve

The Moment I Found Her

T HE TRUTH ABOUT HOW I met Bergen, my wife, is a bit murky. There are intricate bits and pieces to the story, but for now, I'll just say we met online.

Ironically, it was Todd who had encouraged me. He thought it would be good for me to have a girlfriend—a friend to hang out with, someone to talk to. I was desperate for that too. Someone I could really talk to. Someone I could get to know on a deeper level.

But if I'm honest, that wasn't all.

Todd and I had struggled on and off for years. I was beginning to wonder if there were things I could do individually to unlock deeper intimacy in our marriage. Having once had an experience with a woman in my youth, I was curious whether being with a woman again might uncover desires I'd buried for decades.

So, with Todd's permission, I pursued a connection with Bergen.

One chilly October evening, I stumbled unsteadily in my "look how sexy I am" heels through the door of a trendy restaurant.

I looked good.

I felt good.

This would be fun.

I didn't know much about Bergen beyond a photo: blonde, beautiful, kind eyes. My heart slammed against my chest as I scanned the room. She wasn't there yet.

I gave my name at the hostess stand and was led to a quiet table in the corner. I ordered a bottle of wine before even opening the menu.

The door swung open.

A beautiful blonde with an hourglass figure, leather jacket, and pink lipstick strode into the restaurant. Our eyes locked. And something inside me stopped.

Not the polite, oh, there she is recognition. Not even the flutter of a first date. It was something deeper. Primal. Ancient.

It felt like every part of me already knew her.

I didn't just see a woman walking toward me. I saw my person.

My whole body reacted. My heart raced. My stomach flipped. I was in shock. This wasn't nerves. This was something else.

It was as though I had met her before—not in this lifetime, but in others.

I thought of Glennon Doyle's story in Untamed, the moment she saw Abby across the room and felt everything shift. Meeting Bergen wasn't just timing. I felt it at a soul level—an ancient recognition that defied logic. Oh my God, I thought. It's her.

Not just someone to meet. Not just someone to date. Her.

Bergen smiled, pink lips against her pale skin.

"Lane?" she asked.

"Hi," I breathed, standing up. "It's so great to meet you."

It came out more like a question. She opened her arms. I stepped into the hug, breathing in her sweet, earthy perfume and the lingering scent of her shampoo.

I didn't want to let go.

We settled into easy conversation. Bergen talked openly about her kids and her fast-paced, high-pressure job. I saw so much of myself in the details she shared.

She made me feel safe. Seen.

As we talked, it felt like the rest of the room faded. A spotlight trained on us, shrouding everything else in darkness.

It wasn't just chemistry. It was recognition.

Halfway through dinner, Bergen excused herself to the restroom. I followed a few moments later, catching up to her at the door.

"Oh my God, I feel like I can finally breathe," Bergen admitted as we made our way through the restaurant. "I was so nervous to meet you.

Lane, it's so nice to just relax and talk to another woman. I honestly don't do enough of this."

"Me too," I said, trying to restrain my enthusiasm. "Between work and everything with the boys, I've never made space for anyone outside of my family."

"Well, let's change that," she said with a grin.

What happened next—the bathroom stall kiss—is a memory I will always treasure. Not because of the physicality, but because of the feeling: this is home.

A few weeks after that first dinner, Bergen gave me something small but significant—the code to her house.

I'm so grateful for Todd. He had given me a "pass." We had agreed that I could explore this connection and spend time with Bergen. We made plans for me to come over early one morning. The idea was simple: I'd crawl into bed with her before we started the day. A quiet, private moment before the world pulled us in different directions.

That morning, my heart raced as I punched in the code and quietly let myself in. The house was still and dark, the soft hum of the heater the only sound. Bergen was in bed, waiting for me. I stepped into the bedroom and, without a word, slipped out of my clothes, leaving only my bra and underwear.

She lifted the blanket in invitation.

"Come here," she whispered.

I crawled in beside her, the sheets cool against my skin, her body warm and familiar. She wrapped her arms around me and held me close.

At first, there were no expectations. No obligations. Just being held.

But as our breathing slowed and synced, as our hands found each other's skin, something shifted. Yes, we made love that morning. But it wasn't about sex—not in the way I had once understood it. It was a soul-level connection. An exchange of energy. A quiet, wordless conversation between two people who had known each other long before this life.

For years, I had carried everyone else's weight. I had held it together, always the strong one. And now, someone was holding me. Not to take from me. Not to expect anything. Just to see me. To witness me. To meet me where I was, and stay.

When it was over, I lay there quietly, my head on her shoulder, my hand resting over her heart. I didn't want to leave. Not because of the physical connection, but because for the first time in my life, I felt like I had finally come home.

For years, I had moved through the world like a shadow, believing my edges were too soft, my presence too faint to leave an impression. But there in the dim light, watching someone study the map of my skin with reverence, I began to understand that significance isn't always announced with fanfare. Sometimes it whispers through shared breaths and trembling hands.

I learned that power can live in vulnerability—in the courage it takes to let someone witness your unraveling and still choose to stay.

Through touch, through trust, through the gradual dismantling of shame, I discovered that I had been significant all along. I had just been waiting for someone passionate enough to help me see it.

Somehow, some way, while searching for pieces of myself I thought I had lost forever, I stumbled upon my person. And this time, I was ready to choose her. And choose myself.

Thirteen

The Pull

S EVERAL DAYS AFTER MEETING Bergen, I stood at the kitchen counter trying to get my head straight. It's not every day that you try to spice up your marriage by dating a woman. And it's definitely not every day that you develop soul-level feelings for said woman. I wanted so desperately to hang out with Bergen that I had to physically restrain myself from texting her constantly. I had to hold back. I had to be *cool*. The problem was, I wasn't acting cool at home. I was fidgety and impatient, wearing a frown that deepened with every minor inconvenience. Noticing this, Todd began pestering me about why I was acting so sullen. He wandered up to me at the counter and slid a glass of water my way.

"What's going on with you? Are you like … freaked out about the other day?"

"Oh no," I responded, trying to sound casual. "I'm good, work is just busy."

"Well, good thing you have a new friend. You should hang out again."

"Really?" I asked, scrunching my eyebrows together.

"Um, yes? Why not?"

"Okay, maybe I will. That's a good idea. Thanks, Todd."

My heart began to pound as I swiped my phone from the counter and headed into the living room. I plopped down on the couch and breathlessly tapped out a text to Bergen:

Can we meet for a drink or dinner or something?

Several seconds later, she replied:

Sure. Are you okay?

I fired back:

I'm fine. Just need a friend.

We arranged to go out for sushi the next night and see the Taylor Swift movie at a nearby theater. To Bergen, it was just dinner and a movie, but for me, it was more. Every part of me felt the pull of *her*. This meet-up held the butterflies and belly flips of a date. It was another chance for us to sit face-to-face and talk, distraction-free. I sat at the table nervously drumming my nails as she rushed up to me looking frazzled.

"Oh my god, I'm so sorry I'm late. I had a meeting run over. You're sure you're okay?"

"Yes, I'm fine! Let's get you a drink!" I signaled to the waiter with a smile, pointing to my glass of wine and asked him to bring another. "Is work killing you right now?"

"It's officially murdered me."

"I hate that you're so stressed. What can I do?"

"Well, for starters, you can tell me what's going on."

"Okay," I drew a breath, then began picking at the paper coaster my wine glass rested on. "There's nothing *going on*, I don't want you to worry. I just... Bergen, I have really strong feelings for you."

"I like you too," she replied, placing her hand on mine.

"Right, but what I feel is more than that. There's something going on. I can't explain it, I just ... I need you to know. These feelings are big."

"Big?"

The waiter slid a glass of wine in front of Bergen and a bowl of edamame between us before scuttling back to the kitchen.

I leaned forward. "I just feel a really strong connection. I felt it the moment I saw you on that very first night. I know there's Todd and my marriage—I know that, I do. I guess I just need you to know—I feel like there's something else between us. Do you feel that too?" "I mean, what we have is amazing. But it's all very soon and complicated. Both of us are still married. Let's just take this one day at a time."

My stomach dropped. I don't know what I was expecting, but something about this idea felt flat. I swirled my wine and tilted my head. "Yeah, sure. How about we start with a walk tomorrow? Would you be into that?"

"Heck yes, I would. But first, let's eat. I need some food before I head into a room full of Swifties."

The following day, after getting Hunter and Dalton off to school, I hurried into the bathroom to get ready. Bergen and I had agreed to meet at her house to walk the trail in her neighborhood, and I couldn't wait to see her. I threw my hair into a ponytail, swiped on some light makeup, then shoved my feet into my well-worn sneakers. Even as I raced around, I couldn't stop smiling.

"Where are you going?" Todd asked, giving me a kiss on my way to the door.

"To see my new *friend*," I replied. "Are you jealous?"

"Maybe," he said, playfully, waving me off. "Have fun!"

As I closed the door behind me, I swung my keys around my index finger. As soon as I got in the car, I connected my phone to the speaker and began to blast my favorite country music playlist. I tapped my palm against the steering wheel and loudly sang along for the entire twenty-minute drive.

I pulled into her driveway and rang the doorbell. Seeing her again made my stomach flip. It wasn't just how beautiful she was as she tied her hair back in a ponytail, wearing a jacket that hugged her figure; it was something more, something intangible. She wrapped me in a warm hug, then we headed out the door.

"Okay, new best friend, what should we talk about?" I quipped.

"Well, I've got a burning question! I have to ask, what's really going on in your marriage with Todd?"

I tilted my head.

"I'm sorry, I shouldn't have blurted that out. I'm just curious. You two seem so different than one another. And he's supporting you being with me. How does it work with you two?"

"We're definitely different. I don't know. It works, but it doesn't *work*, if that makes sense. I guess it's hard to explain." I took a breath. "We've had a lot of great years. He's my best friend, and we've built a great home-building business together, but we've been lacking in intimacy. We've tried most everything. Couples counseling, etc. Before Todd, I was with a woman for a little while. I guess I always wondered what it would be like to be with a woman again. I thought maybe this might also help my marriage to better know myself."

Dried leaves and twigs crunched beneath our sneakers as we continued to amble our way down the well-trodden path. There, beneath a canopy of towering, bending pines, I felt like I was beginning to access a truth that had been buried deep within me for longer than I can remember. I'd been going through life like a robotic, unfeeling version of myself, *getting through* as opposed to really living. I'd shut down, clammed up, and pushed everything aside that made me, me, in a desperate bid to cling to the picture-perfect life I'd built with Todd. It was as if I'd never considered that there was an alternative until someone entered the picture who forced me to *feel*. These experiences over the last few weeks showed me that there was an entire world I was missing as I'd trained my focus on getting by.

A gust of wind kicked up and ruffled our hair as we walked. The further we moved, the deeper our conversation became. Talking to her felt freeing, like I could just say all the things I'd kept locked up for so long. I didn't have to censor my thoughts—I could tell her whatever came to my mind without fear of judgment. I didn't have to pretend to have it all together or act like anybody else, because she was a human, and she had baggage too.

"Okay, so here's a question for you," I began. "What made you want to connect with me?"

"I guess as I get older, I want to give myself a chance to have all the experiences I never got to have when I was young, you know? I was married young and never really got myself out there. I colored within the lines. Being with a woman had always been a fantasy of mine, so I thought I'd try to do it in a way that felt safe."

"Hold on. You'd *never* been with a woman before this?"

"Well, I met another person online, but it was never serious. So, not really."

"Well, I'd never have known that," I said, pressing my lips together.

As we continued to walk, we talked a little more about Chloe and what that connection had meant to me. We talked about all the ways I had used sex to make men, including Todd, like me. Everything that I had pushed down in my relationship with Todd came to the surface. I shared all the shame I felt that I was a failure at home, an impostor at work, and that I truly believed I was a terrible mother.

"I mean, one of my sons pretty much refuses to share anything with me," I confessed. "And I don't know if it's something I've done wrong or if it's just part of his growing up. I mean, with four boys, a lot gets dropped. I hope he doesn't just feel deprioritized. God, I feel like I'm such a bad mom."

Bergen stopped walking and turned to face me. She looked at me—I mean, really looked at me—and said, "Lane, I hate to break it to you, but you're not perfect. No one is. And your son loves you. You have got to ease up on yourself."

Then, she hugged me.

Soon, we decided it was time to head back to her house and reluctantly turned around.

Our time together felt sacred. My throat tightened as her house came into view. The idea of getting back to real life felt impossibly painful. I wanted to stay in Bergen's space for as long as I could. Yet, our feet were soon at my car, and we were hugging goodbye.

"We'll do this again, right?" I asked.

"Yes!" she replied. "I'll text you later, okay?"

I nodded. "Can't wait."

I turned around and made my way back to my car, my legs feeling like Jell-O, maybe from the long walk or maybe from the avalanche of emotions I'd experienced in talking to Bergen. I slid into the driver's seat as I noticed the smell of her shampoo lingering on my shoulder. I'd finally experienced a glimmer of the intimacy I'd been missing all my life, and realized just how desperately I needed it. The weight of feeling like I had to contort myself to conform to the expectations of others was momentarily lifted. Closing my eyes, I inhaled, as if for the first time.

I deserve this, I thought. *I don't want to carry that weight anymore.* I smiled and revved the engine, then cranked the volume on my music. Something huge had shifted. And I knew deep down that nothing would ever be the same.

Fourteen

Risky Business

B Y THE TIME I met Bergen, leaving Todd had been on my mind off and on for almost a decade. We'd been through so much together—as parents of children with disabilities—and we truly tried to salvage our relationship: marriage counseling, regular date nights, all of it. But we're different people now. While these efforts made our interactions better, they solidified what I knew to be true—I wanted something different for the second half of my life.

I had simply given up hoping that we would ever experience intimacy as *I* defined it: a feeling that transcends time, language, and the physical world. An experience that blends the deep comfort of familiarity with the thrill of eternal discovery. A love that feels like coming home after wandering for centuries, as if your souls recognize each other before your minds do. A connection that's effortless, yet profound, like two puzzle pieces that were always meant to fit. Where you don't need to explain yourself, because they know you—the real you—and you know them. Where time feels irrelevant because even moments spent together hold the weight of forever. With this kind of intimacy, their touch feels familiar, like an echo from another time, yet every moment with them feels new, like falling in love for the first time again and again.

There's no fear of judgment, only freedom—freedom to be seen completely and loved anyway. You look into their eyes and recognize every version of yourself that's ever existed, as well as every version of them. The physical connection becomes an extension of the spiritual bond—something deeper than desire. It's an act of remembrance, a merging of souls that have always been intertwined. It's a balance of peace and passion. A feeling like the universe conspired to bring two people together because it had to. Because their story wasn't finished. Because it never would be.

I remained restless in the knowledge that as long as I was with Todd, I would always be missing something.

Although my marriage to Todd wasn't perfect by any means, on the outside, we retained a sparkling façade. We were the loving parents of four strong, intelligent boys who had banded together to raise awareness for Usher syndrome while juggling our careers and maintaining a beautiful home. If I did anything to disrupt that image—make it known that Todd and I were struggling or, god forbid, divorce him—I would be risking everything I had worked so hard to build: my relationship with Todd's wonderful family, our shared friends, even connections that we'd made through our Usher syndrome awareness work. I had no way of knowing who and what would be left when the dust settled. And I didn't want to—and could never—risk it.

These thoughts swirled through my mind as Todd and I sat side by side at a bamboo counter with a plate of sushi between us. The fluorescent lighting was hard on my eyes, and the cranking AC froze my fingers as I fiddled with my chopsticks. Todd was telling me a story about work, and I tried to engage with it, but my mind was on other things. Not the boys or housework or even ongoing projects at work—instead, I was thinking about Bergen.

At this point, we'd been on a few walks, our conversations venturing deeper and deeper the further into the forest we went. I'd begun to tell her about my childhood—how I'd never felt like I belonged and had always been more comfortable around adults than my peers. As she shared similar experiences, I found it amazing how much we had in common.

"The meeting just went on for so long, I finally said—"

"Todd, I'm sorry," I interrupted him. "I'm not really feeling great. Do you think it's okay if we just head home?"

"Oh. Sure. Of course," he agreed. "We can get this to go. You okay?"

"Yeah, just tired."

He finished telling me his story as he took a couple more mouthfuls of nigiri, packed the rest into a box, then paid the bill. He asked me about my day as we walked to the car. I mustered up as much energy as I could to answer him, but who cared who I met with at work today or what I'd had for lunch? I didn't want to tell him about the papers I graded or how far behind I worried I was falling. I just wanted to go home.

I felt sick. My stomach churned with a sensation that I vaguely recognized as dread. I couldn't help but reflect on my marriage, which

Todd and I were constantly working so hard to salvage. But something about the work we were doing didn't feel right. A little voice in my head whispered, *Call Bergen.* But the responsible side of me immediately shut it down.

The minute we got home, I climbed into bed. The covers were soft against my skin, and maybe it was my imagination, but they seemed to smell faintly of Bergen's lotion. I pictured her stroking my hair and asking, "What's on your mind?" in the soothing way she usually did when we were together. She made me feel heard and seen in a special way. I was beginning to see that our little synchronicities and shared understandings brought out the best side of me.

I shut my eyes and curled into myself beneath the covers. I wanted to disappear. The kind of intimacy that Todd craved had become so difficult for me to provide. I was becoming addicted to Bergen's presence. I craved the softness of her. I craved her lips. I craved *her.* Twenty-five years, four kids, and a lifetime into our relationship, and something was still gnawing at me—I wanted more.

My stomach turned as Todd climbed into bed next to me and rubbed my back. I prayed that his hands wouldn't wander, and strategically shifted my body to prevent him from touching me anywhere else.

I squished my eyes shut as hot tears burned my eyelids. Despite my internal questioning, my feelings for Bergen, my deep desire to really *be* with her, I knew that being with Todd was the only safe way forward. The only way that made sense. I tried to convince myself of that, but the nauseating dread continued. *I'm living a life that's not mine,* it said. *I'm meant for something else.*

As I began to drift to sleep, my mind worked through the ways I could leave. My finances were in order. My suitcases were in the basement. But I'd have to be strategic and extremely cautious. Todd was going to be upset—really upset—and he wasn't going to make it easy for me to leave. There was no way I could leave—I mean, really leave—without a solid, infallible plan in place.

In the week that followed, I went about my routine as normal. I drove the boys to school, shoved piles of laundry into the washing machine, and diligently worked through my overflowing to-do list. Still, expelling the thought of leaving Todd proved impossible. Every time I tried to push it away, it would return with even more intensity. It was like a deep knowing from Spirit, a nudge that kept getting stronger.

When the thoughts began to interfere with my focus, I chose to honor them instead of shoving them aside. I went back through my finances and knew where every single dollar was located. Thinking through how I would deliver the message to Todd, I made a mental list of reasons a separation was a good idea, for his sake and mine. I daydreamed about the peaceful life I could have if I were the only one in control.

In the brief moments when Todd and I crossed paths in the mornings and evenings, I watched him in my peripheral vision, looking for a reason to stay.

The more I thought, the more I convinced myself that I had to leave. Even if it meant blowing up my perfect-on-paper life. None of it was worth the torment of staying, of going through the motions of healing our relationship when it couldn't be pieced back together. A life free from the knowledge that I'd never know true intimacy was worth every risk.

Fifteen

Gut Feeling

As a teenager, when I imagined finding "my person," I always thought I would lock eyes with them and just *know*. Maybe we would have a "meet-cute" like in the movies, or maybe it would just suddenly hit me that someone I had known forever was my soulmate. Of course, I assumed this moment would occur when I was young, and I never questioned whether "my person" was a man. But when I did finally experience the sparks-in-my-chest, twinkle-in-my-eye, body-tingling kind of love, I was over 50 years old, and it couldn't have been less convenient.

Following my walk with Bergen, things didn't get much better. I was enjoying the friendship, I really was. But that feeling of lack and a certain kind of emptiness continued to chase me. Knowing that I was struggling, but still not understanding why, Todd suggested I go away for the weekend to take time for myself, thinking it would fix whatever was causing the dark circles under my eyes. At his suggestion, I seized the opportunity to spend it with Bergen—I couldn't think of anything that would make me feel better.

We left on Thursday, eating junk food and singing along to the playlist she made me in the car. She told me that she had booked us for a massage as soon as we arrived.

Just two hours later, we pulled into the parking lot of the spa and took in our surroundings—trees lined one side of the property, and the other side was open, revealing a vast lake framed by snowy mountain tops.

"Wow," I breathed. Bergen slipped her hand into mine and squeezed.

We made our way to the front entrance, and as soon as we opened the door, we were hit by a wave of warm air that smelled faintly of chlorine and eucalyptus. The person behind the reception desk, a young woman with wavy hair and gemstone jewelry, gave us our room key and told us where to find the massage therapy center, heated pools, and fire pits.

We thanked her and hurried to our room, wheeling our suitcases behind us. The door clicked as we unlocked it, and we abandoned our luggage at the door to throw ourselves on the king-sized bed. She kissed me hard, and I kissed her back harder, then we tore ourselves apart to open the sliding doors to the terrace. I gasped at the breathtaking scenery: the mountains stretched into the pale blue sky and reflected on the shiny surface of the lake, painting a flawless picture of peace.

"We have to hurry," Bergen said, tugging my arm.

We wandered hand in hand to the massage therapy center, a wooden hut with a fireplace in one corner and a water fountain in the other. We were invited to change into warm bathrobes and go into different rooms to recline on white linen beds that smelled of lavender. As the therapist began my massage, I smiled.

The more pressure that the massage therapist applied to my back, the lighter my whole body seemed to feel. Gravity lost its effect on me. I became suddenly aware of all the sounds in the room: the music playing softly from the speakers, the trickle of water from the fountain, and the therapist's long, even breaths.

When the sixty minutes were up, I sat up. My head spun, but my vision was clearer than it had ever been, like I was simultaneously dazed and wide awake. I felt high. So high on love. It was delicious. I exited the room to change back into my clothes, laughing, and Bergen joined in. Our voices swirled into one another like our bodies soon would.

I fumbled with my clothes then wandered to the gift shop next door. I ran my fingers over every shiny object: trinkets, crystals, embossed book covers, and candle lids. I dipped my fingers into all the testers, mixing scent upon scent and reveling in the rush to my senses. Bergen was already waiting for me. She placed something in my hands, and I felt the shape of it—round, cool, and smooth to the touch like metal.

"I found this ring for you," she said, her voice low. "And this bracelet."

I lifted my gaze to meet her face, admiring the shape of her jaw. "Huh?"

"I just wanted to show them to you." She stroked a stray lock of hair behind my ear.

"Huh?" I repeated.

"Oh, never mind. I was just playing around." She took them from me and put them back.

I slid my hand into hers. It felt so safe. "Let's walk around and around,"

I suggested, pointing at the water beyond the window. We headed for the door and did a walk along the water, then I said, "Let's walk over here," when I saw a more secluded area.

Swinging our arms, we followed the well-trodden trail. "You know, you're the best person ever," I said passionately. "I feel like I was totally lost, and you found me. I've never met anyone as amazing and perfect as you."

"I think *you're* the best person ever."

"Do you?" I asked, my smile widening.

We stumbled across a wide green clearing surrounded by bushes that overlooked the stunning view. A fog had begun to move across the landscape, making it look mysterious and even more beautiful. The clearing was laden with rows of white Adirondack chairs adorned with small, colorful bouquets.

"This must be where they host weddings. Let's go up there," I said, pulling her arm and heading down the aisle.

"Why are we going up there?" she asked, laughing.

"Because it's frickin' romantic," I replied.

"It's a lot of work."

"It's four steps!" I pulled harder on her arm.

"Fine," she acquiesced, rolling her eyes.

When we reached the end of the aisle, I kissed her. "Do you think we'll get married here?"

"Maybe," she said, glancing at the mountains, like she was considering it. "But it's a little far for people."

"No, no, no." I shook my head. "We'll make it happen, if it's our dream."

"Oh my god." She widened her eyes. "We *should* get married here."

"Yeah!" I exclaimed, and we burst into fits of giggles.

A cold drop of water fell on my shoulder, and I lifted my hands in the air just as it began to drizzle. Bergen laughed as the droplets landed on her cheeks and eyelashes. I spun around, delighting in it, until I got dizzy and had to sit down. As I reclined in one of the Adirondack chairs, laughing with pure joy, Bergen took out her phone and snapped a photo of me.

We raced back to our hotel room as the drizzle turned to pouring rain. After hopping in the shower, we lay in bed, side by side. We didn't need to have sex to experience true intimacy. We stared into each other's eyes, feeling a wild exchange of energy.

When the intensity of our soul connection had cooled, Bergen pulled out her phone to show me the photo she'd snapped outside, and when I saw it, goosebumps prickled my arms. I'd never seen myself look like that before—so happy, so carefree.

So *alive*.

After this transformative weekend, where I experienced, maybe for the first time, what true love and connection could feel like, I returned home with a heavy heart. I sat in the driveway for a long time, unsure how to re-enter the life I had been living. That weekend had made it clear to me: my life could be different. My heart could feel different.

I realized then that I could no longer continue as if everything was fine. For years, there had been a growing sense of distance and disconnection in my marriage. We had both tried in different ways, but the deep intimacy and shared fulfillment I was craving had become out of reach. It wasn't a matter of blame or fault. We had simply grown apart in ways neither of us could have fully understood at the time.

When I finally walked inside, I felt an overwhelming clarity over me. I had to make a change. I had prepared so many words in my mind over the years, but when the moment came, all I could say was that I needed to go. It was not an easy decision, nor was it impulsive. It was a conclusion I had come to over time, through quiet reflections, difficult conversations, and honest assessments of what was missing for both of us. Before the weekend, I couldn't accept what I knew to be true—I wanted something different for the second half of my life, and I needed to leave.

Though emotions ran high, and it was understandably difficult for Todd to accept, I tried to communicate that this wasn't about any one person or event. It wasn't even about the new relationship that had helped me recognize what was possible. It was about a pattern of unhappiness and misalignment that neither of us could deny.

I understood the fear and frustration my decision caused. I understood the concern that I was making a mistake or acting on temporary feelings. But in my heart, I knew I was choosing growth, not escape.

Even if my future was uncertain—even if it meant being alone—I was ready to honor my truth.

That conversation marked the beginning of a difficult, emotional transition for both of us. But it was also the moment I reclaimed my agency. I wasn't leaving because of someone else. I was leaving because staying meant continuing to deny the life and love I knew were possible.

No matter how things unfolded from there, I held onto the belief that following my intuition, even when it was painful, was the most honest path forward for everyone involved.

Sixteen

Shoulds and Sadness

L IKE MANY WOMEN, MUCH of my life has been ruled by the things I *should* do.

When I was in fifth grade, I knew I should get a boyfriend. When I graduated, I knew I should start a career. When I found a husband, I knew I should have kids. No one sat me down and explicitly told me these things, but the rules were implied—etched into the culture and reinforced through comparison. And I clung to them as if my life depended on it. Because, in some ways, it did. If I failed at any one of them, the shame would surely swallow me whole.

To avoid that fate, I became an expert in performing. In over-delivered. I hustled. I volunteered for every committee. If a family member needed me, I dropped everything. I kept the peace at all costs—even when I was falling apart inside. My "shoulds" ran so deep that I forgot to check in with what I *wanted*.

When I look back at photos from the last few years of my marriage, I can see it in my eyes. My smile didn't quite reach them. There's a faint tightness in my cheeks, a barely decipherable sadness behind the smile. I was trying so hard to convince myself I was fine. That I was fulfilled. That I was lucky. That I *should* be grateful. And I was—but I was also deeply, deeply tired.

There was a time I couldn't admit any of that out loud. Not even to myself. I believed I was the kind of person who shouldn't be sad. Who should have it all together. Who should keep the family happy, the marriage intact, the schedule full.

But the truth is, I was grieving.

Not grieving in the traditional sense of a death or tragedy. Grieving the loss of myself.

I didn't know then that grief could creep in like that. That it could quietly thread itself through the background of my days, subtle but suffocating. I'd wake up with heaviness in my chest. I'd sometimes cry while unloading the dishwasher or driving to Target. I chalked it up to hormones or stress or being "too sensitive." But really, I was sad. Lonely. And I didn't know how to name it.

The sadness wasn't about one event. It was about all the ways I'd lost myself over the years, inch by inch, role by role. I missed the woman I hadn't even become yet. I missed the possibility of me.

But I didn't give myself permission to grieve. I didn't feel entitled to it. Other people had *real* problems. Mine felt like luxury problems—first-world, suburban, privilege-laced angst. So I shoved the sadness down and kept doing what I should do. Until I couldn't anymore.

After telling the boys I was leaving their dad, I felt that sadness in its full force. I lay on Bergen's bed, the sound of her shower water masking the silence of my grief. My throat was tight, and I couldn't loosen it no matter how many times I swallowed. Their confused expressions haunted me.

I *should've* been able to make this work.

I *should've* waited until my youngest was grown.

I *shouldn't* be hurting them.

I'm a terrible mom.

I shoved my face into the pillow and wept. But even as the sadness consumed me, there was a whisper of hope. A flicker of truth. This wasn't about abandoning my family. It was about finally coming home to myself.

The next day, I met with our marriage therapist—someone who had known Todd and me for years. She was still holding out hope we'd make it work, even suggesting polyamory at one point. I looked her in the eye and said, "No. I can't split myself anymore."

I felt a thousand pounds lift off my shoulders.

Later, I found a new therapist. Someone I could talk to about *me*, not just my roles. In our first session, she asked, "What are you most looking forward to in this next chapter?"

I wanted to answer. I really did. But all I could say was, "I don't know."

Because I didn't.

I just knew I *should* spend more time with the boys. I *should* make Bergen feel like a priority. I *should* keep working. I *should* keep everything from falling apart. I should. I should. I should.

"You're using that word a lot," she said. "What if, just for a moment, we ask where those 'shoulds' are coming from?"

It landed. And it scared me.

From that point on, I started paying attention to my inner dialogue. I realized that many of my "shoulds" were actually ways of avoiding shame.

I should go to this birthday party so no one thinks I'm selfish. I should respond to this text right now so I don't seem cold. I should keep working because I don't want people to think I'm lazy. But what if it wasn't shame I needed to avoid but sadness I needed to move through?

So I let myself feel it—the raw, gut-punch sadness that comes with letting go. And in that space—unclenched and unguarded—I found honesty. Not the shiny kind. The messy, tear-streaked, uncertain kind. The kind that says, *I don't have it all figured out, but I'm willing to sit with what's true.*

One day, I drove to see the kids, still unsure of how I was going to be perceived. I walked in with as cheerful a greeting as I could muster, and Hunter barely looked at me. I started to spiral into shame—*I should make this right, I should try harder*—but as I acknowledged these thoughts, I paused. *No,* I thought. *Showing up is enough today.*

That pause became a new practice. Instead of rushing to "do," I started asking, *What do I actually feel? What do I need?* And in asking those questions, I began to slowly rewrite the rulebook I'd followed for so long.

The rules I used to live by didn't allow for sadness. They didn't leave room for complexity. And they definitely didn't encourage stepping outside the lines. But I'm learning to live by different rules now. Ones that say it's okay to grieve something you chose. That growth and sadness can coexist. That sometimes, choosing yourself means disappointing others, and surviving it. That underneath the shoulds and shame and grief, there is a woman who was never broken, just buried.

And she is finally coming back to life.

Seventeen

Being Vulnerable

F OR MANY OF US, sharing our true selves is something that happens gradually over time. Someone forgets a snack for their child, and you reach into your purse for a granola bar; a friend goes through a breakup, and you move mountains to be there for her; your child struggles in school, and you head to the principal's office and demand a conversation. The people who love us get to watch as we chisel our identities through our actions, and although they may disagree with some of your choices—like whether you should have involved yourself in the latest PTA drama—their love for you is never called into question. There is never a moment of doubt over whether they will accept you, regardless of the opinions they quietly hold.

I wish coming out could be that simple. Yet, as we grapple with our sexuality, fear about the thoughts and opinions of others can make us feel paralyzed. The stakes are so high because there is no guarantee of acceptance. Anyone you tell could choose to accept you, tolerate you, or scorn you, and once it's out there, there's no taking it back. I wrestled with this harsh reality as I contemplated how to tell my children that I was leaving their father. I'd practiced the speech years before as my marriage fell apart, thinking I could gather them all on the couch, answer their questions, and end with a group hug. I could never have known the timing would be what it was. Or that it would involve me explaining my sexuality.

Thinking of their expressions shifting from curious to confused to taken aback and maybe even appalled made me sick with terror. I racked my brain looking for excuses—I'd had an emotional year and, since getting a new place of my own, the impending divorce suddenly felt so much more *real*. But the excuses weren't enough to stop me from what I had to do: find the words to confess to them that our family would never be the same again.

I sat on Bergen's couch with my laptop in my lap. I planned on telling the kids that weekend, so I had a few days to figure it out. So, I figured I'd do what I always did when I felt lost: I'd write a list. I closed my eyes and waited for the words to come—after several moments of uncomfortable silence, I accepted they weren't going to miraculously appear from thin air. So, I asked Spirit for help and, suddenly, the words flowed onto the page. It was as if someone else was typing them for me—my fingers just flew. By *Spirit*, I mean the quiet, guiding presence I've come to trust over the years. It's not tied to any one faith tradition or belief system, but rather a sense of something greater—something loving, wise, and deeply intuitive. When I speak to Spirit, I'm tapping into that connection. For me, it feels like an inner knowing that doesn't come from my mind but from somewhere deeper, gentler, but clearer. And when I let go and really listen, I'm often surprised by what comes through.

Later that day, I shared the document with Todd. That was when I realized that there was a fine line between being honest and honoring his feelings. He and I didn't agree on one thing: he felt strongly that the reason I left was because of my relationship with Bergen and the fact that I wanted to be with a woman. But that "truth" didn't feel right to me. I only met Bergen because the marriage had been dissolving on its own. How in the world was I to simultaneously explain to the kids that I was leaving their dad *and* I was in a relationship with a woman? Because that's what it felt like to me—two separate truths.

Good God, I thought, *I'll have to pay for their therapy for the rest of their lives.* Ultimately, I gave in and found a way to blend these messages together. I had faith that my kids, having walked this journey with me, would understand why someday.

One of the most difficult moments of my life was sitting down with each of them to explain two life-changing truths at once: that their father and I were separating, and that I had entered a relationship with a woman.

Because of their different schedules and living situations, I had to have this conversation not once, but three separate times. Each time required its own careful, emotional approach. I knew the news would be unexpected. I also knew it might be confusing or even painful. These were not things I could soften or make simple.

In those moments, my greatest hope was to communicate that while some things were changing, the most important things—the love their father and I shared for them, and our commitment to supporting them—would never change.

The anticipation before each conversation was its own kind of agony. Speaking these truths aloud made them feel more real and, at times, more overwhelming. I also knew that by sharing this part of myself, I was asking them to understand not just a change in our family structure, but a deeper truth about who I was becoming.

Each of them responded in their own way, with their own questions, worries, and—thankfully—grace. There were moments of confusion, moments of surprising acceptance, and even some laughs. What mattered most was that, even in their uncertainty, they never stopped seeing me as their mom.

By the end of that long, emotional day, I was drained but relieved. Sharing my truth with the boys, while painful and imperfect, ultimately reinforced the strength of my love for them. Their reactions reminded me that love can withstand change, even when it arrives in unexpected forms.

As Todd and I drove away in separate directions that evening—he to his home, and I to the new apartment that now marked a fresh chapter—I felt both the weight of what we were leaving behind and the hope of what was to come. We were not a family broken apart, but a family learning to evolve.

Standing in the aftermath of telling the boys about Bergen, I felt something shift inside me. It wasn't just about coming out—it was about finally letting down the fortress walls I'd spent decades building. For years, I'd held every personal truth so close to my chest that they'd practically become part of my ribcage, but now I was learning to open my hands and let my children see what I'd been holding.

This wasn't about maintaining the perfect image anymore—that mask had already slipped, cracked, and fallen away. Instead, I was inviting them into something far more vulnerable: the messy, beautiful process of discovering who I really was. Their acceptance, their love in the face of my truth, felt like finally being able to exhale after holding my breath for years. But I knew this was just the first step on a path that stretched far into the horizon. Like teaching myself a new language, I was only beginning to learn how to speak my truth out loud, how to let people—even those closest to me—see the real me emerging from behind all those carefully constructed walls.

Eighteen

Best Dressed

THEY ALWAYS SAY THAT you never know where you'll end up in life. Considering all of the ups and downs I'd journeyed through, I'd learned this better than most. But when I found myself sitting in a pile of clothes on the floor of my new rental home, which still held the musty smell of the previous owners' dogs, I was overcome by one painful question: *how the heck did I get here?*

Just days after signing a lease on my new home, I started the arduous task of moving in. I had plenty of room, I reasoned, so the seemingly endless truckloads of boxes and bags arriving didn't immediately cause me to panic. But as I started to see everything accumulate in the house, I realized I needed to do a cleanout. I love a good organization spree and this—my first step to reclaiming my life—seemed like the perfect time. I'd begun hauling black trash bags full of my clothes up to the master bedroom, thinking that I wouldn't have to purge much. But as the bags of clothes kept coming, it became clear that this was going to be a major project. I committed myself to only putting things into the closet that I loved. So, I did what any reasonable woman would do and dumped all of the bags out onto the floor.

I thought I would feel inspired, ready to do a cleanout like I've done a million times before. But instead of jumping right in and tackling the task, I froze. I couldn't reach for a single item. I couldn't even make myself move. I stood there paralyzed, feeling my throat tighten around the truth that I almost couldn't bear. I thought I was doing well with all of these transitions, but as I sank to the floor, I realized how wrong I was. When I finally managed to reach for a blouse, the tears began to fall. I felt so much. And I couldn't remember the last time that I truly *felt*.

First, there was the shame. So many of these clothes still had tags on them; not just a few items, I'm talking about dozens. How could I get rid of brand-new things? And how did I stand in stores so many times thinking I absolutely needed these blouses, button-downs, pants, and dresses? What was I doing?

And then there was a tsunami of pain over my failed 25-year marriage. So many of these items reminded me of dinners out with Todd or trips we had taken, or were planning to take. It was as if I were staring down at a pile of carefully curated costumes I no longer needed.

Lastly came the biggest flood of all—the realization that these clothes represented a version of me that no longer existed. There were Lululemon leggings and zip-up sweatshirts, bright, colorful dresses, high-end blouses, and more pairs of designer jeans and toe-crushing heels than I could count. And as I looked down at them, all I could think about was the fact that these items didn't represent who I really was, not even a little. These were pieces collected out of a desire to fit into a life that I had constructed without regard for my true wants or needs. As I diligently pulled item after item from the mound and looked it over, I questioned a different part of myself with each piece.

A red dress with a plunging neckline—*do I even like going to fancy restaurants?*

A too-small pair of Lululemon leggings—*do I even care what moms think of me in the pickup line?*

A pair of sky-high black heels—*do I care about being sexy? What is sexy anyway?*

With each piece of clothing, I began to realize that somewhere along the way, I had completely lost my identity. And this wasn't something that started when I married Todd. I had lived this way for as long as I could remember.

It began in junior high when I started to care deeply about my image. Once I finally started to find my way and make new friends, all I wanted to do was continue to belong. No, I didn't just want to belong; I wanted to be seen as superior, well put-together, cool, happy. That meant building a wardrobe that others would swoon over. I was drawn to anything that promised to make me feel special—jelly shoes, lavender colored zipper jeans, name-brand tops, whatever the latest trend was that week. My mom was the best; she never let on that the last thing she probably wanted to do after a long day at work was drag her daughter to the mall. But there she'd be, keys in hand, ready for another shopping trip. Now, as a mom myself, I understand the bone-deep exhaustion she must have felt, but she never once made me feel like a burden. She was always right there with me, her eyes gliding up and down my body as I emerged from every fitting room and struck a pose.

Shopping became my armor in a world where I never quite felt comfortable in my own skin. There was something magical about sliding into a new outfit, before it had been washed, when it still held that pristine, store-bought perfection. In those moments, walking through the school hallways, people weren't focused on all the things I hated about my body—they were noticing the quality of my clothes, the way I stood out from the sea of sloppy t-shirts and acid wash jeans. I gravitated toward skirts, which, looking back, seems almost comical since everyone else lived in denim, but there was something about the way they made me feel—polished, put-together, like I had my life figured out, even when I absolutely did not. The more obsessed I got with clothes, the more I wanted to spend. My parents had saved for years to buy themselves a BMW, which fit into my image perfectly. I envisioned myself as a character from a blockbuster teen movie; I wanted to be the impossibly popular girl loaded down with bags on Rodeo Drive. I lived my life decked out in expensive clothing and my designer Louis Vuitton and Gucci handbags, and was so focused on my image that I rarely stopped to enjoy being a teenager.

Now that I stood in my bedroom sorting through the mound of clothes, a realization began to take root. These items were evidence of a life that had lived me, rather than the other way around. Each shopping trip had been a desperate attempt to buy my way into belonging, as if the perfect outfit could paper over the cracks in my carefully constructed life. Even now, in my fifties, I was still that insecure young girl, hoping that if I wrapped myself in enough cashmere and costly denim, no one would notice the pain I was hiding. Dressing the part of the woman who had it all together had become second nature—my armor against a world that might otherwise see through the facade of my perfect life to the mess of uncertainty beneath. And, now, as I carefully selected the few items I would keep, I was coming to terms with the fact that I was about to step into a journey that I never, ever expected to take. I was grieving my old life. The weight of it all felt like too much to bear. And now, I was going to have to go inward and meet myself—maybe for the first time—and discover what it really meant to be happy.

Nineteen

My Body, Myself

A LTHOUGH I WAS FINALLY finding my way with someone who made me feel deeply seen, I still had days when I just couldn't get out of bed. I was living a life where my nervous system was constantly in overdrive; it wasn't just digging up old wounds, it was pouring salt in them. I was grieving, but it wasn't just that; I was living in a state of sheer overwhelm. There was too much on my to-do list, and I couldn't seem to get anything done. I was so overcome with shame that I felt frozen in all areas of my life, and I knew I would be able to process these feelings if I could just sit with Bergen and get it all out. But she was busy with work, and I couldn't seem to find the right moment to sit down with her and communicate what was going on. I soon found myself existing under a cloud of pain and anxiety that I couldn't possibly lift alone. That's when I found myself crouched on the floor of the bathroom suffering a relapse of a disease I thought I'd beaten long ago.

I met Gracie in the dorms my freshman year—she lived just down the hall, close enough that we could hear each other's music through the thin walls. We bonded quickly, not just over our love of late-night study sessions and our shared love of junk food, but over something darker that threatened to consume us both.

I had just broken up with a boyfriend when I started spending more time in the dorms, and with that, I was looking for ways to fill my time. There was a nearby walking trail that surrounded Green Lake, and it became my sanctuary. Gracie and I would pull on our workout clothes and head to the trail, at first just for one loop around. The rush I felt after our walks was incredible. It was the feeling that I used to chase on shopping sprees, and I learned that I could find that feeling in the rhythm of our footsteps and in the way my mind would quiet as we circled the water. Soon, I found myself addicted to the rush I felt after our walks. One lap became two, and soon we were signing up for races, pushing ourselves further and further, chasing that feeling of having just one thing in my life I could control.

Exercise started as my salvation—a healthy way to manage the chaos in my head. But like everything else in my life, I couldn't do it halfway. Those seven-mile walks became an obsession, eating up hours of my day until even that wasn't enough anymore. The time it took started causing its own kind of stress, but I couldn't stop. I needed that delicious high, that feeling of being in control of *something*.

I'd grown up watching my mom on a rollercoaster with her weight. She'd yo-yo between a size four and a twelve—weight was always a shadow lurking in our home. So, when Gracie started using laxatives to keep her weight down, it piqued my interest. I didn't want to use laxatives; the idea of that really grossed me out. But I'd heard of people bingeing and purging, which seemed more like something I could handle, even though I was terrified to try it.

One Tuesday afternoon, I decided it was time. I loaded up on all of my favorite foods: pizza, tacos, cake, candy, and cookies. I ate it all until my body was full to a near-bursting point; at first, I was savoring each bite, then I ended up forcing as much down as I could. Afterward, I went to the bathroom; my belly flip-flopped at the thought of what I was about to do. What was it going to feel like? Was it going to hurt?

I gingerly knelt down in front of the toilet, then pushed my fingers down my throat. It was over in mere seconds, and it was uncomfortable, but it wasn't as painful as I'd feared. And when the rush hit me, it was like nothing I had ever felt before. My entire body vibrated, I felt lighter, euphoric, as though I was floating on puffy clouds in a dollhouse pink sky. I was hooked.

I soon became a woman possessed. I wanted to live inside the beautiful feeling of *after.* The purging became a science I could master—it was never about the binge eating, which felt foreign and wrong to my body, but about chasing that feeling that followed. I learned the rules like a twisted playbook: which foods worked best (Lucky Charms were my favorite), the thirty-minute window I had to work with, the exact amount needed to avoid pain. It wasn't about watching numbers drop on the scale; it was about finding those moments of perfect silence in my mind.

There's something that happens when you're in the middle of it, something that reminds me now of being in a hot yoga class, where the heat becomes so intense that your brain can't possibly hold onto anything else. All those spinning thoughts about failure and not being enough, all the stress and pain that usually fills every corner of your mind—they just evaporate. Like a runner hitting their stride, suddenly there's only this moment, this action, this complete and total focus.

The world outside falls away, and in its place comes this strange euphoria, this feeling of finally being in control of just one small piece of your life, even if that piece is destroying you. I guess it's no wonder that I desperately wanted that feeling in the midst of the chaos that had become my life.

For me, the bulimia was never really about food—it was about control. College felt like this endless state of limbo, caught between who I used to be and who I was supposed to become. And if there's one thing I've learned about myself, it's that I can't handle limbo. Even decades later, during those weeks of uncertainty before my divorce, those old urges came rushing back like a tidal wave I thought had long since receded. Back then, just like now, feeling out of control, feeling like I didn't quite fit in anywhere, made me desperate for something—anything—I could control. I wanted to skip ahead to the part where life made sense again, where I belonged. But I've come to understand that you can't fast-forward through the messy parts, no matter how hard you try to purge them away.

That day, when I found myself on the floor of my bathroom, it didn't end the way I feared it would. Finally, when I was able to lift myself up, I grabbed my things and drove through tear-blurred streets to Bergen's house. I sat in her driveway, my hands frozen on the steering wheel, unable to even open the car door. But Bergen—she must have sensed something was wrong because she came outside, pulled open my car door, and wrapped me in her arms right there in the driver's seat. In that moment, surrounded by her warmth and the faint scent of her perfume, I did something I hadn't done in longer than I could remember: I asked for help.

Twenty

Bucking Tradition

I WILL NEVER FORGET the relief that came with marrying Todd. It wasn't the feeling of relishing new love, but the feeling of being *complete* in a way I'd never felt before. There I was with this picture-perfect life, complete with the white picket fence and the beautiful kids who I so desperately loved.

As I left that marriage, I was forced to face a truth that constantly threatened to overwhelm me. My life was no longer perfect on paper. Because no matter how perfectly *me* I felt with Bergen, from the outside I was now living a life that was decidedly different. I was now in a same-sex relationship and, truth be told, I didn't know what the heck I was doing. I found myself standing at the edge of something both terrifying and beautiful, like peering over a cliff into roiling waters. This thing with Bergen wasn't part of any checklist I'd ever made. It didn't fit into my carefully constructed vision of white picket fences and fairy tale weddings, the life I'd been programmed to want since I was old enough to dream. The shame would creep in during quiet moments and mix with the deep-seated fears that had formed in my mind. What will my friends think? How can I even begin to explain this? And my boys? Will this do some irrevocable damage to them as they try to process it?

I've often found myself reflecting on why the universe brought us together in the way it did. For those who may not share the same beliefs, it can be difficult to explain. But for us, it feels as though our connection stretches beyond this lifetime—as if we've known each other before, in different times and different forms.

We both believe in the idea of soul contracts—the notion that before we are born, our souls choose the people and experiences that will shape our journey. It's a way of understanding the deep, sometimes inexplicable bonds we feel with certain people.

Over time, we've talked about how, in this lifetime, our journey together looks different than it might have in the past. This time, we found each other as women—something that has added layers of both challenge and beauty to our story.

Even for those who don't see the world through this lens, I think most can relate to the feeling of meeting someone and sensing that the connection is somehow older and deeper than it seems. That's the feeling we've always had.

In many ways, stepping into a same-sex relationship has felt like learning to walk all over again, with no roadmap and no guarantee that I wouldn't fall. Even though the boys knew and were supportive, every day brought new questions, new uncertainties, and the constant weight of wondering if I was brave enough to handle the blowback that I was certain would come. Standing in front of my bathroom mirror each morning, I found myself rehearsing explanations I hadn't even been asked to give.

But as the months wore on, I started to feel myself relaxing into my new reality. It turned out that beginning to shed my reliance on the *shoulds* in life was one of the most freeing things I would ever do. I'd spent my whole life with long hair that flowed over my shoulders, just because long hair was feminine. It didn't really matter what I wanted—it's what traditional views of femininity dictate. But one day recently, I marched into my hair salon and told my hairdresser that it was time for a big change. Over the next two hours, she chopped my safe, mousy hair into a daring short bob and dyed it platinum blond. I still felt feminine, but in a whole new way; a bold way; a me way.

Then, I took on another task and headed back into my closet, which, by the way, was much less terrifying since the purge. I yanked out over half of the dresses I owned and tossed them into a huge donate pile. I thought I liked dresses, but I still hadn't worn one since moving away from Todd a year ago. In my married past, I wore them nearly every time Todd and I went out on dates, and practically lived in them when we were on vacation. I used to think I loved them, but now I couldn't so much as picture myself wearing any of them. But it wasn't just dresses, it was tops, shoes, skirts and pant suits. Why did I need to keep all of this stuff when it represented a version of me I was no longer connected to?

The truth is, however, wrestling with my femininity and redefining my views on gender expression was just the tip of the iceberg. Bergen and I were now boldly headed into our new lives as a same-sex couple in a world that is unforgiving at best. Whereas I used to be able to hide the fact that I was different, our uniqueness as a couple was on full display. When people saw us together, whether with our families or just out and about, they would immediately know we weren't a traditional couple—we were *gay*. Or they would assume we were sisters (this always makes us giggle). This caused me anxiety because I never liked to share anything with anyone until it was perfect. Every idea, every emotion had to be vetted through an endless series of internal committees before I'd let it see daylight. I'd become an expert at holding everything close—dissecting, analyzing, rehearsing each word until I was absolutely certain it was bulletproof. The thought of sharing something raw, something unfiltered, made my stomach clench with that familiar anxiety.

My heart still races every time I have to present to a room full of people. That old familiar voice creeps in—*who do you think you are? No one wants to hear what you have to say.* The impostor syndrome wraps around my throat like a vice, and suddenly, I'm drowning in self-doubt. Back when I was with Todd, these moments of vulnerability were met with dismissal wrapped in well-meaning words. "You're being stupid," he'd say. "You're a badass." But telling someone they shouldn't feel something doesn't make the feeling go away. What I needed wasn't a pep talk—I needed someone to sit with me in that scary place, to simply say "I hear you" and mean it. For so many years, I'd numbed myself against these feelings, building fortress walls around my heart so thick that nothing could penetrate them. But now? Now, I feel *everything*. Every judgment about my relationship with Bergen, every whisper about being the one who left my marriage, every worry about how my choices affect the kids—it all hits with the force of a tsunami.

I found myself with my guard up, wrestling with the painful truth that we would now be subject to the reality that we were bucking tradition.

Sitting at my kitchen counter every morning, I'd catch myself playing out imaginary scenarios in my head—each one a different version of someone judging us, not understanding, thinking we were *weird*. It's funny how I'd become the screenwriter of other people's reactions before they'd even had a chance to have them. Here I was, feeling more vulnerable than I'd ever been, preparing for battles that might never come. After all, I'd spent my whole life fitting neatly into the expected boxes—wealthy, female, married mom in suburbia. I'd been wrapped in that protective bubble for so long that stepping outside of it felt like learning to breathe different air.

The everyday moments bring the most unexpected questions. Is it weird to go on a double date with a husband and wife? What about work events—do we go together? What does curriculum night at school look like with two moms? Bergen and I navigate these waters carefully, reading the room before we hold hands. In Seattle, we're free to be us. But back in our conservative suburb, we keep a careful distance on our evening walks. We show affection at home with the kids—they've adapted well, casually tossing around "the moms" like it's the most natural thing in the world—but in public, we're still learning how to exist in this space without drawing attention that might make them uncomfortable. Though sometimes I wonder if that's more about our own fears than theirs.

There's something almost comical about trying to figure out the "rules" of a same-sex relationship when you've spent your whole life following the heteronormative playbook. Bergen and I find ourselves laughing about things like who stays home—suddenly, I'm kind of a "stay-at-home wife" for lack of a better phrase—a phrase that feels both foreign and oddly right on my tongue. After years of wrestling with my own trauma around whether staying home shows weakness, I'm learning that maybe these roles aren't about gender at all; they're about finding what works for you and the person you love, regardless of what anyone else thinks. Our family needs one of us at home, so that's what we're doing for now. We're both new at this, stumbling through together, creating our own normal one day at a time, even though I'm still scared.

Letting people see the imperfect, messy truth of who I am terrifies me. It's like inviting the whole world into those vulnerable spaces I spent decades protecting. But there's something powerful in standing in that vulnerability, in finally letting myself be seen, even if my knees shake and my voice trembles. Because the alternative—going back to that numb, walled-off version of myself—feels like a kind of death I'm no longer willing to accept.

Twenty-One

Craving Connection

For much of my life, I shaped myself to be liked. I adjusted, adapted, and anticipated everyone's needs—not because I was weak, but because I thought that was the price of belonging. But as the years passed, something inside me began to shift. I realized that being liked wasn't the same as being known. Approval wasn't the same as connection. And while I had spent decades perfecting the art of being agreeable, what I longed for—what I had always longed for—was to be fully, authentically seen.

For years, I confused attention and approval with closeness. I mistook the validation that came from being wanted, desired, or admired for genuine intimacy. I used sex as a tool for connection, not because I wanted to, but because it was the only path I knew.

But eventually, even I couldn't ignore how hollow that left me.

The desire for something deeper grew. Quietly at first. Then loudly.

And when I met Bergen, everything I had buried beneath decades of people-pleasing surfaced all at once.

This was connection. Real connection.

The kind that doesn't require you to perform or predict. The kind that lets you just be.

For the first time in my life, I felt fully seen—not because I was trying to be agreeable or desirable, but because I was finally allowing myself to be known.

For years, fitting in with the wives of our couple friends was a quiet, exhausting struggle.

I tried. I really did.

When we'd gather at barbecues or holiday parties, I would smile and listen intently as the other moms swapped stories about school events, soccer schedules, and home renovations. They'd share jokes about their husbands or complain about the latest PTA drama. I would nod along, holding my drink and laughing at the right moments, while my mind spun elsewhere—doctor appointments, therapy plans, future what-ifs that weighed far heavier than the latest bake sale.

I remember one particular summer barbecue. The other moms were gathered around the patio table, balancing paper plates on their laps, while the kids darted in and out of the sprinklers. Someone brought up how their son had refused to go to swim lessons, and the conversation turned into a lighthearted competition over whose child was the most stubborn. When it was my turn to chime in, I hesitated. I could have talked about how Conner's teacher called me again that week, or the anxiety I felt waiting for results from the latest vision tests. But I knew that would stop the conversation cold. Instead, I smiled and joked about how my kid never wanted to eat vegetables, as if that was the biggest challenge I was facing.

I became an expert at that—choosing the safe story, the relatable anecdote, the version of motherhood that others could nod along to.

But no matter how hard I tried, I always felt like an observer. The friendships between the other moms seemed effortless. They made impromptu coffee plans and took girls' trips. I was always included, technically, but only when I remembered to reach out, to suggest a time, to keep showing up. I wondered if they sensed my difference, my underlying detachment, or if I simply wasn't as skilled at performing normalcy as I thought I was.

And yet, the solitude I felt in those spaces wasn't entirely unwelcome. I had long since learned how to rely on myself. Alone, I could think clearly. Alone, I could process complex problems—the kind of problems that didn't come with easy answers or casual advice.

In isolation, I found control. I could protect my energy, guard my emotions, and feel a sense of competence in a world where so much was out of my hands. I didn't mind it.

But I still craved connection. Real connection. The kind that didn't require pretending, managing impressions, or minimizing my truth to make others comfortable.

After the separation, that craving became impossible to ignore.

Now, in my fifties, staring at my phone's contact list that suddenly seemed as empty as my new apartment, I had to laugh at the irony. Here

I was, finally ready to build real friendships, and I had no idea where to even begin. The aftermath of my split with Todd had carved deep lines through my social circle—friends chose sides, and most gravitated toward the familiar comfort of our couple-friends status quo, leaving me standing alone on the sidelines.

But something was different now. After years of trying to be the perfect wife, the perfect mom, the perfect friend who never rocked the boat, I'd finally found my center in this unexpected love with Bergen. It was like I'd been building a house from the roof down all these years, and only now had I discovered the importance of a solid foundation. For the first time, I wasn't seeking friendship as a way to prove my worth or check off another box on my life's to-do list. Nor was I content with calling the people I went to events with my true friends. Instead, I found myself dreaming of real connections—the kind where you can show up in sweatpants with unwashed hair and still be met with open arms and understanding eyes.

I could almost taste it: those late-night conversations that meander like hiking paths, the shared bottles of wine that loosen our tongues, the knowing looks across crowded rooms that say *I see you, I get you, you're safe here.* The possibility of having friends who would show up not just for the Instagram-worthy moments, but for the messy, tear-stained ones, too.

It turns out that authenticity is like a magnet—once you find it within yourself, it starts drawing in others who recognize that same truth. I found myself watching Bergen—the easy way she maintained deep friendships, how naturally she nurtured those connections. I started reaching out to people who had always made me feel seen, not the carefully curated couple-friends we'd accumulated over the years, but the ones who knew me before I started building walls. The friends who didn't need me to be perfect, who could sit with me in the mess of who I was becoming.

For the first time in my life, I wasn't trying to collect friends like accessories to match my perfect life. Instead, I was learning to recognize and cherish those rare souls who could look at all my broken pieces and still say, *Hey, I've got you.*

Twenty-Two

Beneath the Perfect Life

A FTER TODD AND I celebrated our 25th wedding anniversary in Costa Rica, I wrote a blog about how hard it is to keep a marriage together when you are parenting children with disabilities. As I wrote it, I steeled myself and tried to count my blessings, truly hopeful that our marriage would survive. I thought we'd overcome the hardest challenges through navigating our kids' less-than-easy childhoods, and we were celebrating twenty-five years of a life together that was wonderful in so many ways.

It was around that time that I decided to embark on writing a memoir. Putting the story of my and my boys' lives on paper gave me an opportunity to reflect on the blessings and challenges I'd faced. The process required me to be vulnerable and open up about a lot of complex feelings: some I didn't know I had, some that centered around my relationship with Todd, and some that centered around my doubts that I was a good mom. As I perched at my desk and watched the page count rise, I was forced to acknowledge that my sons weren't the young boys I'd depicted in my book anymore. They were growing into young men, and in a few short years, Todd and I were going to be empty nesters. For nearly the entirety of our married life, the needs of my children were at the core of my daily routine.

I leaned back in my desk chair as I began to zone out. For once, I was reaching a stage where I could refocus on myself, but what did I *want* for myself? My spine tingled as I considered it. I had devoted almost my entire adulthood to advocating for, supporting, and loving my husband and kids. But under the weight of it all, I struggled to find enough time for everything—enough time for me. So much of my identity centered around being a parent, a wife, the head of a company. If I stripped all of that away, what was left?

To get to the heart of the question, I knew I would need to let myself be vulnerable in a way I hadn't been for years. After nearly two decades of putting others' feelings before my own, I couldn't remember what *feeling* felt like. I had built a wall to section off the parts of Lane that didn't neatly fit into the cookie-cutter life I'd squeezed myself into. Now that I wanted to let her out, I couldn't. The wall was too high and sturdy. Bringing it down would take time and effort, especially if I didn't want it to crumble and take the rest of my life with it.

As I looked into the eyes of the writer I'd hired to help me with my memoir, I tried to verbalize the pressure and anguish that weighed on me to no avail.

"Just try to find a word that describes how you felt in that moment," she encouraged me.

I stared at her, trying to come up with something, anything that truly communicated the heavy, nauseating knot that sat somewhere between my chest and my stomach. I could feel it—it was there. But how could I explain it? By letting myself burst into tears? After a beat of awkward silence, I coughed up, "Bad."

Instead of seeing this inability to pinpoint and identify my emotions as the suppression it was, I turned my frustration outwards, blaming it on the fact that I was used to thinking in a logical, organized way. I was the kind of person who wrote lists and created spreadsheets and stuck to schedules. How did I *feel* in those moments? I never had time to stop and think about it.

I spent my kids' childhoods believing that if I just wrote one more email to the IEP team or reached out to one more person to explain Usher syndrome and deafblindness, the world would suddenly become a better place, some of the pressure would lift from my shoulders, and I'd be able to slow down. Instead, with each email, I became more and more desperate. And numb.

My kids thought it was funny that I lost my cell phone so many times a day and that I couldn't remember anything unless I scribbled it in the notebook I carried around. Now, I see this was all part of me losing myself. After nearly missing my third event in one week, I booked myself for a doctor's appointment. The doctor asked me several questions and concluded that it was probably stress-related—I needed to take some things off my plate. But I couldn't. I was struggling to stay on top of my schedule and to-do list as it was. Not even an hour after my appointment, I was back at work, frantically finishing projects and composing more emails to my sons' schools.

That night, I lay in bed with my back to Todd. My eyes watered with exhaustion and my whole body ached. *I wish things were different*, I thought fleetingly. But before I could let myself sit with that statement and envision what *different* could mean, the issue of the day would intrude, and I'd slip back into problem-solving mode. *If we can just add one more member to Dalton's IEP, he'll have the support he needs and I'll be able to think about other things,* I told myself. But with four kids, I always had some issue or other to fix. I was a hamster and my family was a wheel—my mind had to run at top speed to keep up with their needs. I couldn't come off it because who would pick up the slack? It had to be me. And who cared if I was drowning as long as, from the outside, my life seemed perfect?

The next morning, I woke up devoid of joy and totally lost. I knew at my core I needed to make a change, but I was afraid. Any action I took, big or small, would affect Todd and the kids.

I considered how I would feel if any of my boys were in my situation. If any of them experienced the stress and emotional numbness I was, I'd be devastated. I wanted them to know that they could be their authentic selves—it was okay to venture beyond the safe and known, if that was what their hearts and minds told them to do.

Reeling from this realization, I took the first step: I decided to learn to love myself again. I started saying "no" to things I couldn't handle and used the pockets of extra time that provided to practice meditation, therapy, and affirmations. *I don't need to be perfect all of the time,* I said over and over, trying to make myself believe it. As I did this and the writing of my first memoir came to a close, I took a hard look at the question, "What do I want the second half of my life to look like?" I discovered that, in the deepest part of my soul, even though I was so thankful for the life I had, grateful for Todd, for the kids, and for who I had become, I wanted my future to be different. I wasn't happy. But I really, really wanted to be.

So, I began making changes to my life—gut-wrenching changes. I moved out. I let flimsy friendships fall away. I resigned from my job so I could take care of myself and figure out what was next. And although I knew these changes were right for me, I felt like I'd let down most of the people in my life. But after decades of letting myself down, I finally loved myself again and recognized that I deserved to be loved. I could look in the mirror for more than a few seconds without turning away. I could wear clothes that I liked, rather than for the sake of impressing others. I could laugh without caring how loud I was being. My spark had returned.

When Bergen walked into my life, I knew that I was meant to be with her. A weight lifted from my shoulders every time I was in her presence—I could laugh, cry, open up, and most importantly, *feel* again. I've cried more since I met her than I've ever cried in my life. And it feels amazing. But my happiness doesn't stem from Bergen or the divorce. It's come about because I was brave enough to choose myself, to realize that I can be an amazing mom *and* be true to myself. I don't have to hide my feelings.

I don't regret my twenty-five-year marriage. Not at all. I'm thankful for the laughs and beautiful times I shared with Todd and the lessons that my boys taught me about myself. Motherhood has been my greatest joy. But I'm glad that Bergen looked past my pain on the first day we met and saw that there was light inside me. My life is truly beautiful and has been all along—it just took accepting the imperfections to realize that.

My story, just like all of ours, is unique. It can be messy, chaotic and overwhelming, but it's beautiful and it's mine. If I could change anything, I wish I had realized sooner that I didn't have to lose myself in order to be the best mom I could be. I wish I had learned to be vulnerable from the start.

Twenty-Three

Using My Voice

FOR MOST OF MY life, I believed there was something inherently wrong with using my voice for my own sake. I was loud on everyone else's behalf—advocating for my sons, being a leader at work, heading big projects—but standing up for myself was something I always avoided doing.

When Bergen introduced me to her friends and they asked me what I did for work, I self-censored in the same way I had throughout my marriage to Todd. Don't get into anything that they'll find boring, and don't brag about how you're helping people, I would think. I gave simple answers, then turned the question back on them.

"Wait, why are you doing that?" Bergen said with a laugh during one of these interactions.

"What do you mean?" I asked.

She looked at me, perplexed. "You just shut down."

"Well..." I shrugged. "I just answered the question."

"Honey, you need to work on your elevator speech. You're doing so many amazing things!"

"Really?" her friend asked. "Tell me about it."

"But it's so complicated," I said, shaking my head.

My work was so tightly entwined with the hurt of my past—the challenge of my sons' diagnoses, the difficulties of finding suitable support, the pain of watching them struggle to complete certain tasks and be independent. I never once doubted that it was worthwhile, and although I was often judged for continuing to go to the office despite how badly my family needed me, I never wanted to quit. Explaining all of this and being vulnerable enough to justify my passion was impossible to cover in a five-minute interaction.

It didn't help that we live in a world where people are defined not by who they are, but by what they do. When I was younger, I was one of those people, stereotyping people in certain professions, respecting someone more or less depending on their position in the corporate hierarchy, and basing a person's value on their salary, including my own.

Shame consumed me because I didn't fit into any of the boxes society gave me to choose from. I didn't work in corporate America, I didn't own my own business, and I wasn't a stay-at-home mom. I took a job a few months after I met Bergen, believing that she wouldn't love me if I didn't make money. Compared to her salary, my earnings were nothing. I equated that to mean I was nothing and that, since my job was so difficult to explain, it wasn't worth talking about.

"Do you really think that no one cares?" Bergen asked me as she carried some empty glasses to the kitchen once her friend had left.

I tried my best to express the real reason I found it difficult to talk about.

"But that's not it at all," she interrupted me mid-sentence, setting the glasses on the counter and looking into my eyes. "You know, sometimes, I ask myself, why are we here?"

I narrowed my eyes, looking around the kitchen. "Here? Because we love each other."

"I mean, why are we here?" She laughed lightly. "On this earth. What is our purpose?"

I shrugged. "I don't know."

"Me neither," she confessed. "But I think it's just to be—to exist. And we're doing that."

My stomach fluttered. "But that's so scary," I replied quietly. "That means that nothing we do matters. Why should we even try?"

"Or maybe," she continued, "it's freeing."

I retreated to the living room to sit with the discomfort of the day and think about Bergen's existential questions. Why am I here? What is my purpose? Just being wasn't enough for me—I wanted to help people. So what if I wasn't a director and my earnings were below average? There was no shame in doing what I was supposed to, regardless of whether it was out of the box and difficult for others to relate to.

It finally dawned on me: I'm living my purpose. I didn't know why helping people was my thing, but it was. Why shouldn't I use my voice to talk about it? Not everyone would understand, just like not everyone understood why I left Todd, but those people weren't my real friends. They didn't care how I was or who I was or why I was, so they had no right to dictate my worth or the value of my actions. Maybe I wasn't the director of a successful company, but I was the director of my successful life. And I was going to tell everyone who would listen.

Twenty-Four

Alone, But Not Broken

B Y THE TIME I left Todd, loneliness and isolation were not
new to me. My chest physically ached as I embraced the
familiar sensations that came with facing the world alone, and I was
reminded, once again, of Little Laney as she vied for friendship on the
playground.

It wasn't leaving Todd that made me feel this way—ending that
relationship brought me as much relief as it did grief and I felt freer
outside of the marriage than I had within it. The challenge came when
news of our separation was made public and, one by one, I watched my
"friends" turn their backs on me. In some instances, I knew the reasons
for their actions for certain: they disagreed with same-sex relationships,
or they blindly supported Todd. In others, I could only speculate.
Regardless, it was hard to watch the confusion in their eyes morph
into judgment. I'd choke on my words as I saw the chance of us ever
speaking again slipping away.

With each lost friendship, I sank deeper into a spiral of shame. To be
in a same-sex relationship in my conservative circle, you had to have

courage, yet that courage seemed to elude me. I cringed at the thought of being spoken about in hushed tones at a dinner party or being looked up and down with squinted eyes while running errands.

"Did you hear about Lane?" one acquaintance would say to the other.

"No, what happened?"

Then, the woman would lean in and say, "I heard she left her husband for a woman."

"No, she didn't!" the other would exclaim. "Lane?"

The mental image of her shocked face made me nauseous.

In many ways, I felt as though I deserved it. Of course, everyone would choose to side with Todd. I was the one who had ended our marriage—Todd had done everything he could to stop me from leaving. People thought he was the "victim" in the situation and the one that my "friends" deemed worthy of support.

I knew how they felt because, until a few months ago, I was them. I was the kind of person who would wonder, *How could she not know she liked women? Why did she get married in the first place? How could she hurt her husband like that?* And, *Were the last twenty-five years just a waste?*

Now that I felt sure I was going to be confronted with these questions, I practiced my answers over and over in my head. Sometimes, my answers would be brave—I'd stand up for myself and be honest but firm. Other times, I would apologize on the verge of tears. My certainty that everyone who knew me before the divorce was thinking these things made me afraid to reach out to them, but at the same time, their disinterest in continuing our friendship seemed to be confirmed when none of them reached out to me.

Whereas I only had "couples friends" (people in relationships, who Todd and I hung out with together), Bergen had a handful of close friends that she saw regularly. They were friendships that she had nurtured over the years—people that she could go on trips with, take shopping, and invite for coffee or dinner. Seeing her so surrounded by understanding, supportive people when I had no one made me feel lesser and I asked myself, Why? Why did everyone else have friends and I didn't? Was I so unlikable? What was wrong with me?

To ease some of my loneliness, I took some of the conversations I wanted to have with a friend and typed them into a Word document. I began by introducing the complexities of my marriage, family, and relationship with Bergen, then evaluating them as I would for a true friend: honestly, supportively, and without judgment. I spent some time polishing them, then released them on my blog for the world to see. I felt like I had to be my own friend in these lonely, uncertain times and I hoped at least one other person would read it and be able to relate.

Over a matter of weeks, I received messages from ten people: some I didn't know and some I hadn't talked to in years.

"Oh my God," one woman typed. "I really appreciate your blogs and your vulnerability."

"You've put how I've been feeling into words," said another.

"God, Lane, I was wondering if you were okay," said one.

My heart lightened as I poured my energy into reading and responding to them. We exchanged stories, held space for one another's challenges, and offered our support. These online connections didn't replace the large in-person friendship group I yearned for, but they gave me courage and a spark of hope.

Twenty-Five

Redefining Community

"WE CAN'T BE LESBIANS," Bergen announced to me one day as we were curled up on the couch, watching TV.

"What?" I asked, bewildered. "Why?"

She pressed her lips together. "Because we have no lesbian friends."

"When exactly are we going to find time to do that? And more importantly, how?"

She grabbed her phone from the coffee table and turned it on. "I was scrolling on Instagram and I saw there's a popular lesbian bar in Seattle."

A bar? The last time I'd been to an actual bar, grunge was just coming into style. "Aren't we too old to go to a lesbian bar?"

A crease appeared between her eyebrows, and I kissed it. "I don't think there's an age limit," she replied.

"Well, we really can't fit it in right now," I said apologetically. "Things are fragile with the boys, and your work schedule is insanely full. It was a fight getting ourselves time off for Valentine's Day, let alone—"

She raised her eyebrows.

"No." I sat up straighter. "No! It's our first Valentine's Day as an official couple..."

"And what better way to celebrate than among our people! Let's do it!" Bergen beamed.

She stared me down.

"Really?" I contemplated it.

"Why not?"

Because we have a brand-new relationship to nurture, I thought. I was still trying to have a decent relationship with my ex; I was trying to cultivate and retain new friendships; I was trying to support my boys through the tumultuous divorce; and I was making an effort to speak to my mom more. How was I supposed to keep everything moving smoothly and build new relationships in the lesbian community?

"You were just telling me how you felt isolated," Bergen reminded me. "Wouldn't it help to have other queer people in our circle?"

"I guess."

"Then, let's go for it. We can celebrate Valentine's Day traditionally next year."

I pressed my lips together, nervous, but excited.

Two weeks later, Bergen and I walked into the trendy lesbian bar like we were tiptoeing into our own future. The space buzzed with Taylor Swift songs and the gentle clicking of beads against tables as small groups of women made friendship bracelets under dim lights. We were easily the oldest ones there by decades, clutching our tequila sodas like security blankets as we claimed the last empty table in the corner. No one spoke to us, everyone wrapped in their own little worlds, but somehow just being in that room, surrounded by couples who looked like us, felt like exhaling.

Later that night, our wrists clacking with handmade bracelets, I realized something profound: community isn't something you can force or chase down. It grows organically when you plant yourself firmly in your truth and let it take root. We didn't need to desperately seek out "our people"—they would find us naturally as we lived authentically, no longer hiding who we were or who we loved.

The real key to connection, I was learning, was having the courage to be seen. Once I stopped trying to curate the perfect image and started sharing my real self—through blog posts, chance encounters at bars, or unexpected conversations—the right people began appearing in my life like wildflowers after rain. Some were old friends emerging from the past, others were strangers whose eyes I caught across crowded rooms, and many were people I never would have imagined connecting with. But beneath our surface differences, we all shared the same core truth: we were all just trying to be a little less alone, all hoping to find people who would see us, hold space for us, and remind us that we belonged somewhere in this vast, complicated world.

Part III

Coming Home to Myself

I had rebuilt the outer pieces of my life: left a marriage, raised four incredible boys, stepped into advocacy, finished a PhD, and started to feel like myself again. But there was still one piece I had been avoiding—the deep inner knowing that I was being called into something more. Not more success or more roles to take on, but more wholeness. A coming home to myself. This section of the book is about that homecoming. About what happened when I let go of logic and leaned into healing fully. About trusting the nudges, the visions, the healing that couldn't be explained
but
transformed me all the same.

Twenty-Six

Love, Light, and Letting Go

The Threshold and the Meadow

T HERE WAS A TIME not long ago when I thought healing meant fixing what was broken. I spent years collecting tools, information, strategies. I read books, managed services, built plans, and advocated fiercely. I knew how to survive. I was good at it.

But at some point, I realized I wasn't being asked to do more.

I was being asked to be.

To pause. To feel. To trust myself enough to stop controlling everything around me and begin tending to what was happening within me.

That realization didn't come from a single epiphany. It was a gradual unfolding. A noticing. It came in the quiet moments after the storm, when the house was still, the advocacy meetings were over, and the grief had settled into something quieter but just as heavy. And in that stillness, a new kind of knowing emerged.

It started in a meadow.

Not a real one, at least not at first. It was a vision that came to me during a guided meditation. I had been trying to meditate for weeks, but it always felt impossible. My mind wandered. My body fidgeted. I'd get annoyed and abandon the practice before I ever got still. But something about this session was different.

I closed my eyes, trying to stay present with the practitioner's voice. And then suddenly, I was there.

A wide-open field stretched before me. The sun filtered through tall grass. There were wildflowers scattered across the landscape: lavender, buttercup, Queen Anne's lace. The breeze was gentle. I could hear the distant rustling of leaves and the slow hum of the earth. It was breathtaking.

And then she appeared.

My grandmother.

She wasn't young or old—she was just... her. She sat on a rock beneath a tree, as if she'd been waiting for me all along. She smiled. Not the kind of smile that expects anything—just love. Unfiltered, uncomplicated love.

I walked toward her and felt my whole body begin to settle. My breath deepened. My shoulders relaxed. She reached out and brushed a strand of hair from my face, just like she used to when I was little.

And in that moment, I knew something I hadn't let myself believe in years: I was safe. I was loved. I wasn't alone.

That meadow became my sanctuary. A place I could return to anytime the world felt too loud, too sharp, too much. I started every meditation by walking through that meadow. Sometimes my grandmother would speak. Other times, she would just hold my hand or place a hand on my heart. She never rushed me. She never asked me to be anything other than who I was.

That visualization practice became more than a tool. It became a lifeline. A way to reconnect with parts of myself I had buried beneath the busyness of surviving.

And for the first time in years, I started to ask:

What if there's more to healing than getting through it?

What if there's another way—one that begins by coming home to myself?

Reiki and the Awakening of Energy

After the meadow came Reiki.

I was skeptical at first. I had always believed in science, structure, research—the concrete and explainable. But something inside me was stirring, asking me to move beyond what I could rationalize. I was tired of being in survival mode. I didn't want more strategies or systems. I wanted peace. I wanted rest. I wanted to stop bracing for the next blow and finally soften into something else—something whole.

My first Reiki session wasn't what I expected. I lay fully clothed on a table in a softly lit room, unsure of what I was even doing there. The practitioner was kind and calm, with warm hands and a quiet presence. She didn't ask me to explain my grief or justify my pain. She just asked me to breathe.

As her hands moved gently over me—sometimes touching, sometimes hovering—I felt a shift. It wasn't dramatic. It didn't even feel "spiritual." It felt like warmth. Like someone turning on a light inside a dark room.

Then the tears came.

Not loud sobs, just quiet, steady tears rolling down my cheeks. I couldn't have told you why I was crying. But something inside me was being witnessed. Released. I felt held, not just by her hands, but by something bigger.

That session opened a door I didn't know existed. I started to receive Reiki regularly. Then I began to study it. I wanted to understand the energy I had felt. I wanted to offer that same kind of presence to others. Eventually, I trained and received attunements so I could practice Reiki myself. It wasn't about becoming a healer; it was about learning to hold space, first for myself, and then for others.

Around the same time, I began to explore other healing modalities, not out of a desire to fix myself, but from a deep longing to reconnect.

I tried sound healing with crystal bowls, tuning forks, and chimes. At first, I felt silly lying on the floor while someone waved instruments around my head. But then I felt the vibration in my chest, my limbs, my throat. I could feel my energy shift—subtle, but real. The sound seemed to shake loose the fear I didn't know I was still holding.

I experimented with chakra balancing, breathwork, and insight Reiki, where I'd set intentions or ask for guidance before a session. I started using crystals, affirmations, and daily journaling to reconnect with my intuition. I found power in simple rituals—lighting a candle, sitting quietly with my hand on my heart, whispering: I am safe. I am enough. I am home.

I also explored plant-based medicine in a ceremonial setting, where I felt deeply connected to spirit and to my ancestors. This experience was profound—not because it made my problems disappear, but because it reminded me that I am more than my roles, more than my responsibilities. It helped me see that there was something sacred within me all along. I had just been too exhausted and guarded to notice.

For years, I had lived from my head. These practices helped me come back into my body—to feel things I'd buried, to release the tightness in my chest, to hear the messages my body had been whispering for years.

Nourishment, Sleep, and the Sacred Ordinary

While I was deepening my spiritual practice, I realized something else: I had spent so much time working on my soul that I had forgotten my body needed healing, too.

For years, I'd treated rest, food, and movement as luxuries I couldn't afford. I skipped meals or ate whatever was quick. I functioned on broken sleep and adrenaline. Exercise was either punishment or another item on a to-do list. And if I had a spare hour? I filled it. With advocacy. With emails. With guilt.

But when I began this deeper healing work, I started to crave slowness.

Grounding. Simplicity. Not everything needed to be profound. Sometimes, healing looked like drinking water and going to bed on time.

I hired a personal trainer—not to chase weight loss, but to build strength. To feel capable again. We worked slowly, with intention. She taught me to track how I felt in my body, not just what I could measure. I learned to appreciate what my body could do, not just what it looked like. I learned to rest between sessions, to fuel myself with protein and greens, to listen when my body said, please slow down.

Nutrition became another act of self-love. I stopped skipping meals or relying on caffeine to power through the day. I started paying attention to how food made me feel. What energized me. What grounded me. I didn't follow a rigid plan. I just tuned in. I gave myself permission to eat without shame, to nourish without restriction. Food became part of my healing, not something to control, but something to honor.

Sleep, too, became sacred. For so long, I wore exhaustion like a badge of honor. I prided myself on how much I could handle, how little I needed. But that was just trauma in disguise. Once I started prioritizing sleep—real, restorative sleep—I began to dream again. I began to wake up without dread. I stopped falling asleep mid-sentence or forgetting why I walked into a room. It felt like waking up from a fog I hadn't known I was in.

I also returned to therapy—this time not to "fix" a crisis, but to tend to myself with curiosity and compassion. I found a therapist who didn't pathologize my spirituality but saw it as part of the whole. We talked about boundaries, nervous system regulation, childhood wounds, and self-trust. We talked about joy—how hard it was to feel it without guilt, and how necessary it was to claim it anyway.

These traditional forms of healing—sleep, food, movement, therapy—weren't separate from the energy work I was doing. They were an extension of it. Reiki taught me how to listen to my body. Therapy taught me how to honor my emotions. Nutrition and rest taught me that I am worthy of care even when nothing is urgent. And movement taught me that strength is born in the slow, consistent return to myself.

Healing wasn't either/or. It was all of it. Spirit and science. Ritual and routine. Letting go didn't mean floating away. It meant grounding down.

It meant saying:

This body is mine.

This life is mine.

And I'm finally ready to live it fully.

Soul Memories and Releasing Shame

There was one fear I couldn't shake—one that had lingered in the background of my healing, even as I practiced Reiki, nourished my body, and found comfort in daily rituals.

It was the fear of being too much.

Too sensitive. Too spiritual. Too intuitive. Too emotional. Too "woo."

This fear wasn't just about others judging me. It was about a deeper, older fear—one that didn't seem rooted in this life at all.

That's when I began to explore.

I was curious, but nervous. I had spent most of my life in evidence-based spaces: research, education, data. And yet, my intuition told me there was something I needed to uncover, something buried beneath logic that had been holding me back.

During the session, I was guided into a deep meditative state. What followed was surreal.

I found myself in another lifetime. I was a woman, quiet, strong, and connected to nature. I worked with herbs and energy. I helped people heal. But I was feared, misunderstood, punished. I saw images of isolation. I heard the cries of women silenced. I felt the weight of being cast out.

In that life, I had died alone. Silenced. Afraid. Carrying shame for gifts I never asked for.

As I relived those moments, I wept. Not just for that version of me, but for every time I had dimmed my own light in this life out of fear that I'd be misunderstood or abandoned. The shame that lived in my cells made sense now. It wasn't just mine. It was old. Ancestral. Carried forward. And ready to be released.

What followed was a deep peace. I felt like I had retrieved a part of myself that had been waiting patiently in the wings. A part that no longer needed to hide.

Soon after, I did a visualization with my practitioner—one that changed everything.

She invited me to imagine my soul family—the people who had

journeyed with me across lifetimes, the ones who had always loved me. I closed my eyes and pictured myself standing in the center of a vast circle. All around me were familiar souls: my children, my partner, my grandmother, friends, guides I couldn't name but instantly recognized.

The scene was quiet but full. I felt a hand tug at my shirt and looked down to see a small child, frail, innocent, wise. I knelt and pulled them close. I didn't need to know who they were. I just knew I had loved them forever.

That moment stayed with me. It reminded me that I am never alone. That I am deeply supported—seen and unseen. That even when life feels disjointed or painful, there is a thread of love that connects every chapter, every version of me.

These spiritual experiences didn't replace the hard work of healing. They deepened it. They helped me understand that my intuition wasn't something to fear or minimize. It was something to trust.

And when I began to trust that part of me, everything else began to shift.

The fear lessened. The shame loosened. The voice that used to say you're too much began to say you're coming home.

The Integration and the Invitation

Letting go was never about surrendering the life I had built. It wasn't about walking away from the people I loved or abandoning the strength that had carried me this far.

Letting go was about softening my grip on control. On perfection. On the belief that I had to hold it all together, all the time.

It was about unlearning the idea that my worth was tied to how much I could endure. Or how invisible I could make my own needs for the sake of others. It was about realizing that surviving isn't the finish line—it's the starting place. The portal to something more.

But here's what no one tells you about healing: it's not just about breakthroughs and releases and big "aha" moments.

It's about integration. It's in the way I talk to myself when I forget something. The way I pause to breathe instead of rushing. The way I light a candle and place my hand on my heart, whispering, You're safe. You're allowed to rest.

It's in my nightly gratitude practice with Bergen. It's in how I eat to nourish, not punish. In the walks I take with my feet on the earth, just to remember I belong here.

It's in choosing joy, not as a denial of hardship, but as a reclamation. A declaration that I am worthy of light, even after everything.

I still have hard days. My body still remembers pain. But I'm not fighting it anymore. I'm listening. I'm offering compassion. I'm honoring the wisdom that's been there all along.

Because that's the most radical thing of all:

To believe that healing isn't something we must earn.

It's something we are worthy of—by birth, by breath, by being.

This chapter doesn't mark an ending.It's a turning point.

The start of something softer. Something deeper. Something real.

An invitation to live from alignment. To love without armor. To let go—not of who I've been, but of who I no longer need to be.

Twenty-Seven

Buried Feelings

LETTING MYSELF FEEL MY emotions was not an easy thing for me to start doing. The wall I put up as a child acted like a dam, and I feared that bringing it down would result in a catastrophe that I couldn't recover from. There were so many things I yearned to feel—love, belonging, acceptance—but letting them in meant letting other things in. Things I'd built a life around avoiding.

When I left Todd and entered into a relationship with Bergen, I let the pent-up wave of emotions crash over me. I cried more in that one month than I had in my entire life. My eyes were constantly red and puffy, and my cheeks were taut with dried tears. As freeing as it was to let the wall come down, I was simultaneously assaulted by a torrent of negative emotions: grief, fear, and shame.

I emerged from the wreckage as a new person, mentally and physically. I moved to a different place; my kids started going to a new school; I began a new relationship. It was hard to fully wrap my head around all the changes that had taken place. Just thinking about it made my chest tighten and my mind spin.

God, did I do the right thing? I'd ask myself, resting my heavy head in my hands.

One day, as I was sorting through a box of photographs from when my sons were small, I locked eyes with myself looking at the camera and paused. I distinctly remembered how that version of me felt—anxious that Conner's vision was getting worse and stressed about the endless tasks she had to stay on top of. My head spun as I was transported back there. Although I'd learned to ride the wave of my emotions in the present, the past still had the ability to submerge me. It was as if I had to make up for suppressing myself for so long.

One of the things I had to face when I opened myself up to my feelings for the first time was the challenge of identifying my emotions. Sometimes the source of the sensation in my chest, stomach, or throat was difficult to pinpoint. When this happened, I learned to sit with myself for a moment and ask, Is this sadness? Is this fear? Is this anxiety?

By labeling what I was experiencing, I could finally verbalize my emotions and share them with Bergen. "I feel a lot of shame today," I told her after replacing the lid on the box of photographs. "I feel like I'm not a good mom."

"Okay," she replied gently, without judgment. "What would make you feel better?"

I thought about it for a moment as I rose to my feet. "I feel like I should spend more time with them. Maybe when they get back from school, I can take them for ice cream?"

Previously, I would have pushed that feeling down and avoided it until it was replaced by something else. No one would ever know if I was ashamed, sad, or scared. Now, I had the courage to face and express it. Bergen didn't try to talk me out of my emotions or jump into problem-solving mode, offering unhelpful suggestions. She simply acknowledged that she'd heard me and asked what I needed to feel better.

I wasn't the only one who had days like that. One day, I came home from work and called out, "I'm home!" When I didn't receive a response, I checked the living room and kitchen, but she wasn't in either of them. Eventually, I found her curled up in bed with her hoodie over her head as if she were taking shelter from the world.

"Are you hooding up again?" I asked.

"Yeah," she mumbled.

Although we had different ways of dealing with our emotions, we both had the tendency to go within. Sitting with our feelings was the first step to owning them. Avoiding hurt was what got me into an unhealed place to begin with. Now, I see how negative emotions, although uncomfortable and sometimes painful, are necessary—they're part of the human experience.

When I had the wall up, I did it for the sake of not hurting others. I worried constantly about what everyone else was thinking and feeling: my teachers, my parents, my friends, my sons. I never gave myself a single thought—surely as long as everyone else was happy, I would be happy. It didn't occur to me that by prioritizing everyone else's needs,

I was hurting myself.

As a result, I have grief and trauma that may heal, but won't ever leave me. I will always have sudden memories of bad moments from my past—flashbacks that will take me back to the stressed and anxious place I once put myself in. I am moving forward, but I am still struggling to move on.

I can confidently say that I'm in a much better place thanks to my healing journey, but I also recognize that had it not been for all of my experiences, I never would have met Bergen or gained the courage to leave my marriage.

Despite the fact that I'm in a better place, I'm still not fully tuned into my emotions all of the time. Once, when I was in the kitchen with Bergen, I felt something unpleasant and unfamiliar stirring in my body. Bergen was asking me a list of questions about our plans for the week ahead, and I found myself feeling less and less willing to answer each time. Eventually, I started offering one-word replies.

"What just happened?" she asked. "You just closed up on me."

I grappled with the sensation inside of me. Frustration? Overwhelm? Anxiety? I couldn't find the word to explain it. I couldn't organize my thoughts enough to let her help me. "I don't know," I confessed eventually.

She looked me up and down. "Something happened. It's okay—you don't have to tell me, but something's up."

I shrugged. "Are you okay?"

"Yeah," she said. "I just feel like we disconnected. That's all."

We sat in silence for a while, then I said, "I think something triggered me, but I don't know what. I can't really communicate it just yet."

"That's fine." She sighed. "Talk to me if you want, but come here. Do you need a hug?" We put our foreheads together and stayed like that for a moment, connecting wordlessly. She didn't force me to tell her what was going on. She didn't press me to tell her what would fix it. She gave me the space to feel everything I needed to feel, and just her steady presence helped my discomfort begin to fade.

If emotions were easy to acknowledge, everyone would confess their feelings and no one would remain unhealed. The crisis of the human experience is that even if we have the best intentions, we will inevitably hurt one another sooner or later. But suppressing our thoughts—pushing them down—is the most harmful thing we can do in the long run. We have to let one another see the difficult parts of ourselves. We have to be willing to weather the storm if we want to survive the flood.

Twenty-Eight

Perfectionism

O UT OF ALL THE tendencies I've struggled with in my life—people pleasing, obedience, overthinking, etc.—perfectionism has been the hardest to overcome. It crept into every little thing I did, from choosing the right outfit to being the hardest worker. Any task had to be handled seamlessly, without a single mistake, or I'd feel like a complete failure. It wasn't that hard to do when it came to the small stuff: forms being filled out correctly, projects being completed carefully and on time, events being hosted properly and carefully. But soon my perfectionism began to spill into my bigger life goals: my house, my marriage, my kids. Before I knew it, my happy vision of the perfect life turned into a façade that I had to frantically keep up.

Until I just couldn't anymore.

To change my perfectionist habits, I had to redefine the word "perfect." To me, it meant trying my best. It meant doing whatever was "good enough." It meant being unapologetically human. My life was perfect because it wasn't. I didn't always finish my to-do list, my relationships had their ups and downs, my house could get messy.

When I left Todd and announced my love for Bergen to the world, the façade I'd been maintaining for years finally dropped. Friends and family saw me cry—some for the first time. And along with that grief came relief. The second I realized I didn't have to pretend anymore, I released my death grip on perfectionism. I let friends wait inside the door when I hadn't had time to clean. I ordered takeout more often to make time for self-care. I even confessed to the people in my life that I was struggling. The trick, it turned out, was not letting go of wanting perfection for myself, but letting go of my desire for other people to think my life was perfect. And miraculously, my world didn't crumble. My load lightened. I finally felt like I could breathe.Sitting at my desk with Bergen standing behind me, her hands on the back of my chair and eyes glued to my laptop, I watched her wrestle with the familiar temptation to slip into perfectionist mode. We were planning a family trip, and I'd practiced choosing a hotel that was just "good enough," without spending days overthinking it. Bergen was having a harder time.

"It's just not what I had in mind," she said, gesturing to the hotel on my screen.

"The rooms are right next to each other, and it has a pool," I replied. "That will work for four nights!"

"I don't want two rooms," she protested, her forehead crinkling. "And it's not even that close to the airport."

"It's a nice place," I promised, scrolling my mouse so she could see all the pictures.

She chewed her lip. "Did you check all the hotels in the area? Why don't we try Airbnb?"

I rolled my eyes. "Oh my God, no."

"You know I'm a maximizer," she said. "If we're going to go away, we're going to make the most of it. I want everything to be absolutely perfect."

I turned around and locked eyes with her and grasped her hand. "But they won't be."

"What do you mean?" she said, her eyes narrowing.

"Something challenging always comes up." I squeezed her warm fingers. "And that's okay. It's a better story if it's not perfect—"

"It's not, though." She shook her head, standing up straighter. "If my daughters are tired and miserable after traveling and your boys don't have everything they need—"

"We'll live," I interrupted her. "I've been on a lot of vacations with a family of six, okay? And, trust me, it's pretty unlikely that there isn't going to be some sort of meltdown or argument. Someone is going to fall down the stairs or get upset about something."

"So, we should do all we can to prevent that." She took her hand away from mine and navigated the mouse to the top corner of the screen to open a new tab.

"Sure, to an extent." I shrugged. "But something messy is going to happen anyway, and that doesn't mean you've failed at planning."

"I just want everything to be perfect," she mumbled, typing "Airbnb" into the search engine.

I knew the feeling well, but I also knew how free I'd felt when I'd finally released it. "There's no such thing as perfect."

"Yes, there is," she replied, a small smile on her face.

"No," I argued.

"Yes."

"There's only perfectly imperfect," I said. "And I like it. I like messy."

"Oh, no, no, no." She stopped her scrolling to frown at me. "Not messy."

I threw my head back and laughed.

"Here. It's minutes from the airport with a pool." Bergen scrolled down. "The kids can have space when they need it, and we can take time for ourselves. Look, there's even a fully equipped kitchen." She pointed out the list of amenities. "See? I plan for every contingency."

"Yeah, yeah." I sighed, spinning from side to side in my desk chair. "Whatever."

I switched seats with Bergen and rested my hand on her back while she booked the Airbnb with glittering eyes. It worried me that she was intent on managing our family's emotions. It was a moving goalpost. I wanted her to feel a sense of achievement and know she was good enough without having to meet an impossible goal.

It struck me that Bergen's perfectionism presented differently from mine. Whereas I wanted other people to appreciate how perfect my life was from an aesthetic and aspirational standpoint, Bergen wanted everyone to feel good. I wanted to control my life, and she wanted to control everyone's experiences. It didn't matter how well-equipped the Airbnb was or how meticulously she planned the itinerary; she could never predict whether someone would be struggling or anxious about something.

The situation made me realize how much progress I had made in letting go of my need to make everything perfect. My nights weren't filled with overthinking my choice, my finger wasn't sore from scrolling, the time I spent looking didn't seep into my other tasks. Now that I'd learned how to accept "good enough," how to relax rather than feel the need to control everything, I wanted others I cared about to experience the same thing. I wanted to model being laid back in my relationship and with my children. Not everything can be optimal all of the time. And that's okay.

Twenty-Nine

Getting Back On My Horse

WITH ALL THE CHAOS of my marriage to Todd ending and my relationship with Bergen beginning, I was too focused on building my new life to return to the things that brought me joy in my old one. Growth was about newness and fresh starts, right? It didn't make sense to cling to my past—even the parts that were working for me. I lost myself in packing and planning, forgetting to look back at the progress I'd made. Everything felt like it could be different—improved in profound ways.

When Todd and I bought our ranch in Washington state three years prior, I knew I wanted to fulfill a childhood dream of owning my own barn with not just one or two, but six horses. Looking back, I can only chuckle. Other than some trail riding experience on vacation, I knew nothing about horses. I had no idea how to care for them or what a halter was, and absolutely no idea how to ride. All I knew was that I felt called to figure it out, and I soon became determined to do so.

My early days of working with horses are a blur. My hands shook as I led them from their barn to the field, and my forehead tensed as I read and reread the instructions on how to mix their feed. My own lack of knowledge and experience made me clench my fists. I'd brought up four boys—why did taking care of horses feel so hard?

Riding was the part I was most looking forward to and the part I was most determined to do well. With the help of a qualified friend, I tacked up one of my horses, Blue, with all the correct equipment and used a step stool to swing myself up. Hunter and I then headed on a trail ride with my friend.

As we made our way out, Hunter started to ride faster. Blue wanted to follow. I didn't know how to slow him down. One moment I was secure in the saddle, the next I was tumbling through air, weightless and disoriented. There was a sickening flash of white light as my head smacked against the packed earth. The world spun violently; the taste of copper flooded my mouth.

I managed to right myself, my fingers fumbling for my phone in my back pocket. My vision blurred around the edges as I tapped Todd's name. His voice sounded distant, underwater. Twenty minutes later, he was helping me into his truck, my legs wobbling beneath me. At the urgent care clinic, fluorescent lights stabbed my eyes as a young doctor with concerned eyes diagnosed what I already knew—a concussion.

Before the fall, I had signed Hunter and myself up for a trip of a lifetime—to go horseback riding around the Ring of Kerry in Ireland. Now, I felt uncertain to ride my own horse, let alone those in another country. I was deathly afraid of getting back on Blue. It took me months to work up the courage to mount him, and even then, I hardly dared ride around the field.

Instead, I sat on Blue, taking deep breaths and trying to get my anxiety in check. I was working with myself to reconnect to him; to somehow quell my fear so that I could move forward. But I still felt stuck.

In an attempt to gain confidence and learn what I needed to, I finally decided to hire someone to teach me and booked a horseback riding crash course. The trainer showed up at my house in riding gear and a low, blond ponytail. She greeted me with kindness before making her way to Blue and softly petting him on the side.

"Your horse can feel all of your emotions—and I mean all of them," she said. "You need to relax and be present, even as you're just walking into the barn."

I tried to follow her advice, releasing the tension in my body by shaking it out before each ride, mimicking the stance I took in meditation. But, still, Blue seemed to sense something was wrong. Was it possible he knew I was stressed out and in my head? Could he tell I was in fight or flight mode, afraid of falling off? As I tried to coax him around the field, he stubbornly refused to walk alongside me and constantly stopped in his tracks.

"What's wrong with him?" I asked with a huff.

"Try to relax your body," my trainer encouraged.

"This is me being relaxed," I insisted.

It was the best I could do. I couldn't understand that Blue was more attuned to my feelings than I was—he knew me better than I knew myself. He could sense the anxiety rippling beneath my skin, the tension I carried in my shoulders. Animals don't lie and they don't pretend. My beautiful horse was simply responding to the storm inside me that I'd become expert at hiding from everyone else.

The process was frustrating and sometimes felt impossible. There were mornings when I'd arrive at the barn wondering if I'd ever feel truly comfortable in the saddle again. The concussion had healed, but the fear lingered, wrapping itself around my spine, threatening to choke what little confidence I had left. Still, I was determined to make this work. If I could learn to quiet the chaos in my mind, if I could reconnect with my body and truly feel the ground beneath my feet, maybe I could ride my horse again without that toxic anxiety. Maybe I could finally understand what it meant to be free, not just in the open field with Blue's powerful body beneath me, but in every corner of my life that had felt constricted for too long.

Over time, I found my way back to myself and forged an unbreakable bond with Blue. I ultimately did make it on the trip around Ireland, and through some miracle, I survived and learned a lot about riding, humility, and my limitations, along the way. Things that I could bring back to my own barn—things I could bring back to Blue.

As the sun rose over the hill each day, I'd walk down with my hands in my coat pockets. The ambience of the horses' sighs, stomps, and distant birdsong would douse me in peace. Blue would meet me at the fence when he saw me arriving, and he'd nudge the air until I gave him pets and neighed impatiently while I mixed his food.

One evening, after I fed all six horses, refilled their water troughs, and mucked out the barn, I took a seat and put my head in my hands. My day had been hectic and challenging as always, running from one task to the next with a never-ending sense of urgency and I needed the peace and solace. I heard a puff of air, like a short sigh and lifted my head from my hands just enough to look toward the barn. Blue was hanging his head over the barn door, peering at me. His big, black eyes met mine and stayed there. Instead of getting up or hiding my face again, I looked back at his.

What do you know about my life? I wanted to ask him, but something in his gaze told me he knew more than I thought. My heart overflowed with warmth for the innocent creature—it was a connection that I'd never experienced with an animal before.

I see your pain, he seemed to say, *and it's going to be okay.*

That evening changed a lot for me. My fears around horses dissipated, and I became better at sensing my emotions' impact on them. Spending time in the barn and fields became my favorite part of the day, and riding got easier and easier. That barn—it was home. Those horses—they were my family.

When I made my decision to leave Todd, things slowly began to change. Riding stopped being a priority for me as the only life I'd ever known fell spectacularly apart. I poured my energy into feeling the torment of emotions that I'd been closed off to my whole life, and with that, I began navigating the many complex issues that came about as a result.

As I said goodbye to my marriage, my home, the life I once knew, the time finally came for me to say goodbye to my horses. One by one, I rehomed them, until the only one that remained was Blue.

I found a wonderful buyer for Blue and arranged to trailer him to his new home. But the day before he left forever, a feeling tugged at my insides, giving me pause. I drove to the ranch to see him, give him pets, and say goodbye in my own way—alone. As I left the car, he met me at the fence as he always had. He tossed his head until I placed my hand on the bridge of his nose. Tears filled my eyes, falling as I tried to blink them away.

"I can't rehome you," I said, petting him as I began to cry.

He snorted as though to say, *No, you can't.*

"You've taught me so much, Blue."

I pressed my face into his warm neck and inhaled his familiar scent—sweet hay and earth and something uniquely him. I'd lost so much already: my marriage, my home, my sense of who I was supposed to be. The thought of losing Blue too made my throat tighten until I could barely breathe. How could I say goodbye to him now, after all we'd been through together? He'd carried me through the darkest period of my life, not just on his back but with his unwavering presence. When everything else had crumbled around me, Blue had remained constant, teaching me that sometimes strength ebbs and flows, but it never really leaves you.

At that point, I didn't know whether I would be able to keep Blue long term, but I didn't care. I reached into my pocket to get out my phone and called the buyer to cancel. I knew that Blue was meant to be with me. There was still so much I had to learn about myself and who I really was—and he needed to be part of that journey.

It had been months since I'd ridden him, but I headed into the barn and tacked him up, feeling the same jitters that I had three years prior.

As I stepped onto the stool to swing myself onto his back, a doubtful voice in my head asked, *Am I capable of riding? Will I fall off? Am I relaxed enough, or will Blue sense the anxiety I feel?*

I pulled myself up, settled into the saddle, and deeply inhaled. Everything I loved about riding came rushing back to me—how freeing, how attuned, how connected it felt. As we began to walk and then trot, it became clear that I was messy. I had a lot of work to do to get back to where I was before—both in my riding skills, and my own healing. But, in that moment, I was grateful—grateful for what I had learned about myself and grateful for Blue and his patience with me.

When I thought I had to say goodbye to every part of my old life in order to welcome in the new, I was missing one vital truth. My new life is all about love, both from and for myself and others. It doesn't matter whether that takes the form of a partner, a child, or a horse as long as it's genuine and complete. Selecting parts of my old life to carry into my new life requires consideration and bravery. But I can overcome my fears as easily as I got back on my horse—with solace, determination, and gratefulness. The love and healing that stems from that decision is worth it.

As the sun dipped below the tree line, casting long shadows across the field, I finally understood that life isn't about perfect execution; it's about showing up authentically, even when you're scared. Blue's hooves beat a steady rhythm against the earth as we made lazy circles in the golden light. Here, with the wind in my hair and my body moving in rhythm with Blue's, I felt true connection to myself and to the new life that awaited me just beyond the pain.

Thirty

Letting Joy In

The Unraveling

B Y THE TIME I turned fifty, I was worn thin from holding it all together. I had become the kind of woman others looked to for strength. I kept our family afloat. I coordinated the chaos well, scheduled the therapies, ran a nonprofit, worked full time, advocated in D.C., and kept smiling through the exhaustion. There wasn't space for much softness, let alone space for me.

But underneath all of that—the stability, the dedication, the role I played so well—was a version of me I hadn't let breathe in years. And when I met Bergen, it wasn't just about chemistry or falling in love. It was a mirror. A moment that forced me to look at what I had stopped allowing myself to feel.

She saw me in a way I wasn't used to being seen. I didn't have to be "on" with her. I didn't have to perform. There was no mask. No expectation. And as much as it scared me, it also woke me up.

It would be easy to say that everything changed in that moment, but the truth is, this awakening had been building for years. It didn't arrive as a thunderclap. It came in pieces—longing, restlessness, numbness I couldn't explain. Little signs I brushed aside because it was easier to keep going. Easier to survive.

But something shifted. I couldn't unfeel what I had felt. I couldn't unknow what I now knew.

This isn't just a coming-out story. It's a coming-home story.

Yes, I came out as queer. But more than that, I came out of hiding—from everyone, including myself. I had spent so much of my life trying to be what others needed, what was expected, what looked good from the outside. And I was tired. Not just tired in my body, but tired in my spirit.

The day I admitted out loud that I wanted something different, something *more*, was the day I started living honestly. I wasn't trying to destroy my past—I was trying to honor my future.

Todd and I had shared a full, rich life together. We raised four boys. We built a family with deep roots. But somewhere along the way, I disappeared. My needs, my desires, my voice—they had taken a back seat to survival. And I didn't want to keep disappearing.

People asked, "Are you sure?" But how do you explain the relief of being seen—*really* seen—for the first time? How do you describe the way your body exhales when it finally feels safe enough to be fully present?

Coming into my queerness wasn't just about sexuality. It was about trust. It was about honesty. It was about permission.

Permission to be more than what others expected.

Permission to be a woman in her fifties who still had growing to do.

Permission to be alive in her own skin again.

What Followed

At first, I didn't even have the language for what I was feeling. I was scared of what it might mean, how it might ripple through the life I had built. I worried about what others would think, especially my children, my family, and the community I had worked in for years. It felt safer to keep the peace, to stay in the structure, to shrink myself just enough to keep everything intact.

But something inside me had shifted. Once I allowed myself to see the truth, I couldn't unsee it.

There was no one dramatic moment where I stood up and declared, "I choose myself." It was quieter than that. I noticed that I was laughing again. That I looked forward to things. That my body felt lighter. That I didn't need to brace myself just to get through the day. Joy started to creep in, almost shy at first, like it wasn't sure it was allowed.

Being with Bergen helped unlock that. She didn't demand that I change; she just welcomed who I already was. She met me with curiosity and care, and in her presence, I felt free to stop performing. Not just for her, but for everyone. I stopped explaining. I stopped editing myself. And that's when the becoming began.

What followed wasn't easy. There was grief. There was fear. There were conversations I never imagined having. There were people I love who didn't understand. But there was also something else—something steady and grounding: relief. Relief that I wasn't pretending anymore. Relief that I could finally exhale.

I think I had believed for a long time that joy was something reserved for other people. That my job was to make sure everyone else was okay. But somewhere along the way, I began to understand that I was allowed to be okay, too, not just okay, but fulfilled. Curious. Loved. At ease in my own skin.

Leaving the life I knew wasn't about chasing a fantasy. It was about finally telling the truth. About what I wanted. About who I was. About how I wanted to feel.

It took me until fifty to get there. But I did. And I wouldn't trade it for anything.

Thirty-One

The Day I Dated Myself

T HE IDEA CAME FROM a class I was taking at the time. The instructor invited us to try something bold, something nurturing, something that might feel a little uncomfortable in a good way. She said, "Take yourself on a date."

Not a "run errands alone" kind of outing. Not a productivity break dressed up as self-care. A real date. One with intention, curiosity, and presence. A day where the goal wasn't to get things done, but to be with yourself in the same way you would be with someone you love.

At first, I laughed. Then I went quiet. *What would that even look like?* I pondered.

I had spent so many years putting everyone else first—my kids, my marriage, my work, the mountain of expectations that always seemed to grow faster than I could climb. I could barely remember what I actually liked to do just for me. But the idea stirred something. It felt tender. A little thrilling. A little sad. And very much necessary.

So I said yes to myself.

It was a Tuesday, and the house was still. No appointments. No carpool. No looming deadlines. Just me, a soft gray sky, and a sliver of time I hadn't planned to have. I sat with it for a moment, that rare and unexpected quiet, and I contemplated what it would look like to spend this day loving myself.

Not fixing. Not performing. Not accomplishing. Just... loving.

At first, I hesitated. It felt strange to even consider taking a whole day to myself, not to catch up, not to check off tasks, but simply to *be*. But I leaned into the idea like I might lean into a gentle hug from someone you're learning to trust.

I got dressed slowly, deliberately. Pulled on my comfiest jeans, a soft cardigan, and warm socks. I tucked a book into my bag—not because I thought I'd read it, but because I liked the idea of carrying stories with me.

Then, I drove into town and parked near my favorite little bookstore. It wasn't a big place, but it smelled like paper and cedar, and the music playing was always just soft enough to wrap around you. I didn't go in with a list. I simply wandered. Ran my fingers along the spines. Let myself be pulled toward a novel I'd never heard of and a poetry collection with a cover that made me feel something I couldn't name.

From there, I walked to a quiet café. I ordered a tea—Earl Grey with oat milk—and took it to a small table by the window. Outside, the trees swayed gently, like they were exhaling a breath they'd been holding too long. I wrapped my hands around the warm cup and just sat there. Not thinking. Not scrolling. Not analyzing. Just... being.

After tea, I drove to the forest trail I used to walk when the kids were little. I hadn't been there in years, and I'd almost forgotten how soft the moss was, how the air felt cooler and cleaner under the canopy of pines. I walked slowly, without a goal or a destination. I let the hush of the woods settle into my bones. Let the birdsong brush past me like a whisper.

It was so quiet. So alive.

And I realized that in all the noise and motion of the last few years—raising children, making hard choices, advocating, loving, grieving, beginning again—I had forgotten what it felt like to be in my own company. Not alone because I had to be. But alone because I *chose* to be.

And in that choice, something softened.

I wasn't trying to prove anything.

I wasn't trying to fix anything.

I was just with myself. In rhythm. In breath. In peace.

Taking myself on a date wasn't about being brave. It wasn't even about self-care in the traditional sense. It was about remembering that I'm a whole person, not just a caregiver, not just a partner, not just a name on someone else's paperwork. I'm a woman who likes bookstores and tea and the smell of the forest after it rains. And I deserve to spend time with her.

I came home that day with a new book, muddy shoes, and a calm I hadn't felt in years. Not because anything big had changed, but because I had remembered something small and sacred:

I belong to myself.

Not Shy, Not Anxious

A S MY OUTER WORLD began to shift—my marriage ending, my children growing more independent, new love unfolding—there was another transformation happening quietly underneath it all. A change less visible, but just as profound. I was not only rebuilding my life. I was remembering my soul. The healing that followed wasn't just practical. It was spiritual. It became the foundation for everything that came next.

For most of my life, I believed endurance was enough.

I wore it like a badge of honor—the ability to carry impossible loads, to anticipate every need before it was spoken, to organize, soothe, and persevere. I didn't realize how disconnected I had become from myself. My mind and body had adapted to meeting constant demands, but the cost was silence—the quieting of my own voice.

Motherhood, especially parenting children with disabilities, required everything of me. Advocacy, caregiving, building a life where my sons could thrive—this became the rhythm of my days. And in the process, without even noticing, I stopped tending to the softer, sacred parts of myself. I stopped listening to my body, to my own needs, to the gentle nudges of my intuition.

I thought holding it all together meant I was succeeding. But holding it together is not the same as living. And it's not the same as becoming.

Eventually, my body started telling me what I had long ignored. The weight I carried, the exhaustion that sleep couldn't fix, the heaviness in my chest—these were not just physical symptoms. They were signs. Something deeper was calling for my attention.

At first, I didn't know where to begin. All I knew was that I couldn't keep living disconnected from myself.

The first steps were simple. I tended to my health in new ways, learning how to care for myself, not as another item to cross off my to-do list, but as an act of restoration. I moved my body not to change it, but to reconnect with it. I let myself pause before saying yes to things. I no longer answered every text right away. I took short walks without my phone. I let myself breathe.

When my body resisted pushing harder, I listened. When my heart felt tight before a decision, I paused. My intuition didn't arrive in thunderclaps. It arrived in whispers.

It was a whisper that told me: this isn't fear. This is knowing. It was a whisper that said: you're allowed to trust yourself.

For years, I told myself I was shy. Or socially anxious. I felt different, like I didn't fit in as easily or seamlessly as everyone else. I would leave social gatherings exhausted, needing days to recover. I struggled to keep up with surface-level conversations. I thought something was wrong with me.

But the truth? I wasn't shy or anxious. I was intuitive. I was highly sensitive. I was someone who felt the world deeply—someone who could pick up on emotion, energy, tension, and beauty all at once. But because I hadn't been taught how to recognize or honor that part of myself, I shut it down. I laughed at jokes and nodded at things I didn't understand or care about and tried to blend in to meet the expectations of a world that celebrated doing over being.

Once I accepted that I wasn't broken—just intuitive—my life changed. I began to notice how my body communicated with me. A pit in my stomach. Shallow breathing. A tightness in my throat. These weren't signs to ignore—they were information. When I learned to listen to these signals early, I stopped needing full-on meltdowns or shutdowns to know something was wrong.

When I was married, it was hard for me to access my intuition. I was too busy. Too tired. I was stuck in survival mode, always caring for someone else. I dismissed the pit in my stomach as "just anxiety." I brushed off that tightness in my chest as stress. But really, it was my body trying to tell me something. It was my knowing, rising up to guide me, saying, You're allowed to speak your truth. You're allowed to ask for more. You're allowed to trust yourself.

But I didn't believe it. Not yet.

Then, not long after I left my marriage, while I was on a cruise with Bergen and her daughters, I received an email that made my heart skip. I got a job offer in higher education finance. Fumbling with my phone, I shared the news with Bergen. I was thrilled. I knew what I needed to make to live independently, and this job met that criterion. I'd be working for someone I liked, with colleagues I respected, and the work itself was familiar. I even had the final interview on a university campus, surrounded by students and the buzz of possibility—something I had always loved.

That day, lounging on the cruise ship, surrounded by people I loved and cared about, with a future that was coming together, I felt seen. Wanted. Capable. And in a moment when I was still rebuilding my confidence, that validation meant everything.

But as I started telling more people that I had accepted the job, I noticed something strange: I didn't feel excited. In fact, every time I talked about it, a piece of me went quiet inside. I started having trouble sleeping. I'd lie in bed at night and feel a persistent unease. Not because I didn't want to work, but because deep down, something felt off.

I began to meditate every morning, desperate for clarity. I'd sit quietly and ask, Tell me what I need to know. One day, a vision came clearly into my mind: two paths.

One path had a sign over it that said "NOT YOURS" in big, bold letters. The other path was clear, light-filled, and open. And suddenly, it clicked. I had been asking for guidance but ignoring the answer. I had been pretending I didn't know, because the truth felt inconvenient. But the truth was—I couldn't take this job. Not because I wasn't capable. But because it would pull me out of alignment. I knew it in my body, even if my brain protested.

It wasn't just about the hours or the commute. It was about choosing a life that allowed me to be the mother, partner, and healer I was becoming. Taking the job would have required me to abandon myself.

So, I did the hardest thing I could do. I decided to turn it down.

I felt physically sick just thinking about the call I'd have to make. The hiring manager had known me for twenty years. How could I let him down like that? I imagined him frustrated, disappointed, even angry, and I feared he'd never speak to me again.

But Bergen helped me process it. She asked, "What would you want someone else to do in this situation? Would you want them to show up to a job that would drain them? Or to be honest and protect their peace?"

That conversation helped me find my courage. I called him, and with a shaky voice, said, "I'm sorry, but I can't accept this role. I have to prioritize my family and my healing right now."

The moment I hung up, I felt it. Peace. Ease. The anxiety was gone. That clarity—that yes, this was the right decision—washed over me. My body relaxed. I could breathe again. And that was the first time I truly saw what it meant to live in alignment.

The decision not to take that job changed more than just my calendar. It changed how I made decisions. It deepened my trust in myself. It was also a turning point in my relationship with Bergen.

Suddenly, we had to ask hard questions. Would she carry more of the financial load while I focused on healing and family? Would we be okay? It was scary, especially because our relationship was still new. We hadn't even finalized our divorces yet. But we chose to trust each other. And that trust created space for me to fully step into the people we were becoming.

Now, I live with more intention than ever before. I don't rush. I don't overexplain. I don't say yes when my body is screaming no. I know what alignment feels like—and I protect it fiercely. Intuition has become my compass. It helps me understand when something is meant for me, and when it's not. It helps me know what's mine to carry, and what I can lovingly set down. My life is more peaceful, not because it's free of challenge, but because it's grounded in truth.

I trust my timing. I trust my body. I trust myself. And that trust has become my greatest strength.

Even in Fear, I Knew

T HERE WAS A TIME when fear ruled me quietly. It didn't storm in, waving red flags. It whispered. It disguised itself as self-doubt, people-pleasing, and perfectionism. It told me to wait. To stay small. To not speak up. To not rock the boat. And I listened.

I built a beautiful life with a steady rhythm, carefully curating what the world saw. I made decisions that looked smart, responsible, admirable. But beneath it all was a hum—an undercurrent of something I couldn't quite name. A quiet panic. The feeling that I was holding my breath, hoping no one would notice I was barely holding it all together.

Fear doesn't always scream. Sometimes it just keeps you busy. Busy doing what's expected. Busy chasing certainty. Busy convincing yourself that this is enough.

But there was a deeper truth inside me that I hadn't yet allowed myself to hear. And it took everything falling apart for me to finally listen.

When I left my marriage, I was flooded with fear. Just the kind of fear that makes you question whether you're making the right choice—the kind that rattles your identity. I feared hurting the people I loved. I feared judgment. I feared ruining my children's sense of stability. I feared losing the only version of adulthood I had ever known. I feared waking up one day and realizing I'd made the biggest mistake of my life.

Fear accompanied me into every room, every conversation, every quiet moment in the months that followed. And yet, so did something else—a knowing that I couldn't go back. That once I'd cracked open the truth of who I was, there was no way to reseal it.

I didn't feel confident. I wasn't brave in the way people like to define bravery. I was terrified. But I kept going. The most honest choices I've made in my life weren't made in the absence of fear—they were made *with fear sitting right beside me.*

I remember sitting on the floor of my new apartment, the echo of its emptiness louder than I expected. I had wanted this. I had chosen it. But in that moment, all I felt was panic. I had no idea what would come next. I didn't have a plan, a clear five-year vision, or a list of perfectly calculated steps. What I had was a quiet whisper in my soul that said, *keep going.* And I did. I kept going through nights when my heart ached with guilt. When I wondered if I'd done irreparable damage. When I second-guessed everything. When I watched my kids' faces and wondered how they'd carry this into their own stories.

I kept going through the awkward newness of becoming someone I didn't fully recognize yet. Through the mess of letting go and the beauty of beginning again. And little by little, I started to realize something: fear had always been with me, but it wasn't always the enemy. Sometimes, fear was just the signal that I was stepping outside of who I had been told to be—and toward who I actually was.

Fear showed up when I was about to grow; when I was about to step into deeper love; when I was about to take up space; when I was about to claim a life that felt like mine. I started to understand that being afraid didn't mean I was weak—it meant I was alive. It meant I was human. And it meant I was paying attention.

Now, when fear comes, I invite it to walk beside me, but I don't hand it the keys. Because even in fear, I know who I am. Even in fear, I trust my voice. Even in fear, I take the next step. Even in fear ... I know what's true.

Thirty-Four

The Path I Never Expected

I F YOU HAD TOLD me ten years ago that this would be my life, I would've laughed. Or cried. Maybe both. Not because it isn't beautiful, but because it was so far outside the vision I once clung to that I wouldn't have been able to imagine it.

Back then, my life was a carefully choreographed routine of basketball games, Costco runs, mowing the lawn, and driving four boys all over town. Our family ran like a well-oiled machine—Todd and I were a team, each managing parts of the chaos. He handled the grocery shopping and home maintenance, and I handled most of the behind-the-scenes logistics: IEP meetings, schedules, the emotional work of caregiving, and the thousands of unseen decisions it takes to keep a family moving forward. I didn't cook—I still don't, really—but I baked when the mood struck, and occasionally tried to make a "real" meal (usually with one of the boys nervously hovering nearby, ready to jump in if I started to burn something).

Todd used to tease me that grocery shopping with me was torture because I got so excited and distracted by every new product in the aisles. Now, my version of grocery shopping is home delivery apps and bribing my boys to help. And they do—because they know I hate it. They come with me, steer the cart, and help me get through the overwhelming maze of it all. I miss the ease of how things used to be sometimes. I miss the clarity that came with being a wife in a very traditional sense of the word. But I don't miss who I had to be to stay in that life.

And now? Now I live in a home filled with four teenagers—two boys and two girls. Before, I was the lone woman in a household of five boys. There were drones getting stuck in my hair, lightsaber battles breaking out in the living room, and endless debates over who got the last Eggo waffle. I loved it. They even used to throw me "princess parties," complete with hand-drawn signs and paper crowns. But now, the energy in the house has shifted—there's more laughter, more Taylor Swift, more mascara tubes on the counter, more shared clothes and shared secrets. It's different. It's chaotic. It's beautiful. And it's hard.

Blending families is complicated. I knew that going in. What I didn't know was how deeply it would challenge my sense of identity, of belonging, of control. As a mom of four, I thought I knew what I was doing. I didn't expect the grief that would sneak up on me when one of Bergen's girls needed something I wasn't sure I should provide. I didn't expect the pang of jealousy when I watched Bergen comfort one of her children in a way I wanted to comfort them. And I didn't expect the tenderness I would feel when one of the girls called me for help with something small: needing a ride, help with an outfit, or advice about a friend. Stepparenting isn't linear. It isn't tidy. But I've learned that love doesn't have to be tidy to be true.

There have been nights when I've cried to Bergen, wondering if I was doing it right—if I was loving them enough, respecting them enough, stepping back enough, showing up enough. Some days, the only thing I could hold onto was the fact that I showed up. Again and again.

And at the same time, my life outside the home—my purpose—has continued to evolve. Earlier this year, I was invited to speak at a press conference alongside our state senator, sharing my story and advocating against proposed changes that would devastate children with disabilities and their families. I stood in front of cameras and microphones, my hands steady, my voice clear, and I spoke on behalf of families like mine. Next month, I'll be traveling to D.C. to continue that work at the national level.

Sometimes, I think back to the shy girl sitting against the wall in her fifth-grade classroom, afraid to speak up, afraid to be noticed, afraid to take up space. The same girl who used to cry before giving school presentations. That girl had no idea she'd grow up to be a confident advocate, standing shoulder to shoulder with lawmakers, helping shape policies that affect thousands. She had no idea that one day, she'd walk into a room not to shrink, but to stand tall and lead. And honestly? Sometimes, I still can't believe it either.

But maybe the biggest shift of all—the one I never saw coming—is how I've started to take up space in my own life. For decades, I made myself smaller to keep the peace. I dimmed my light to avoid overshadowing anyone. I was so used to being needed that I forgot how to need myself. And now, I'm rediscovering what it means to be in relationship—not just with others, but with myself.

I used to think I had to do everything. That if I didn't, the world would fall apart. But in this new chapter, I've learned that it's okay to lean on others. That love doesn't mean self-sacrifice. It means that sometimes, asking for help is the bravest thing you can do. That joy is worth chasing, even if it comes with risk.

Bergen and I still have our moments—we're raising four teenagers, after all—but every time I look over and see her unloading the dishwasher while I attempt to cook (and our teens laugh at my poor kitchen skills), I'm reminded of how far I've come. How different this version of partnership is. How much softer I've become. How much fuller life feels.

I never thought I'd be here. But I'm so glad I am.

Thirty-Five

Opening Up

I REALIZED HOW LONG I had been living in shame. All the challenges I'd faced as a child and a parent had seemed like my fault—because I wasn't good enough, because I had failed. I asked God, *Where did I go wrong? What did I do to deserve this?* And I couldn't understand why He wouldn't give me a straight answer. Then, I learned I wasn't the one to blame. And my whole mindset shifted.

Loving myself and living my truth came more easily once I put pen to paper to write my truth, but it became fully possible for me the moment I let myself love and be loved. Opening up to Bergen—sharing my own emotions and being receptive to hers—was the turning point. The point at which I began to ask, *Why am I so hard on myself? Why am I treating myself differently than I treat other people?*

Sensing the change in me, my friends decided to open up more, to be more honest and vulnerable about what was on their mind and how they were feeling. I sensed the change within myself too. When

I was closed off and cold, I vibrated white energy: hollowness, like a raw canvas that wasn't ready for painting. Now, I vibrated pink. It was warm, cozy, and safe. My friends now knew that they could tell me anything and I would be nurturing and forgiving.

"I don't know what I'm doing," one of them had confessed over coffee one day. I placed my hand on her shoulder. "Lane, I'm scared."

Whereas I might have hesitated or responded with a blank stare in the past, the right words came to me now. I didn't have to muster them up or figure out what she wanted me to say. I simply had to listen and instinctively respond. She could be vulnerable because she knew I wouldn't judge her. She could show her true self because she knew I wouldn't criticize. Something within me had shifted. These words consistently came to me and I repeated them internally, like affirmations:

I'm strong.

I'm good.

I'm deserving of love.

Although my intention of becoming myself and healing had a literal, emotional meaning, I explored alternative definitions as well.

What clothes did I want to wear? Did I want to have more energy? What kind of partner did I want to be? What kind of mom did I want to be?

Some of the answers were obvious once I confronted them. I already knew I was a better mom when I worked and held boundaries. Other questions, like "How do I want to look?" were much harder to answer. I had to feel okay about being different. My new life was untraditional—but it made me happy, and that was the most important thing.

It used to matter to me whether I pulled up to my sons' school in a Land Rover or a Ford and whether I had a big house on a ranch with six horses. Now, I was grateful to have a car that was reliable and a house that felt like home. Until I released my desire to "keep up appearances," I had no idea how much of a burden it was. I felt like I wasn't only fighting to present myself a certain way, but to justify it to anyone who asked. I exhaled especially hard on my next breath, appreciating the absence of that pressure. It felt good to know my worth wasn't attached to worldly things, like belongings or the type of job I had. *I'm not here to make money,* I thought, *but to help people.*

I still felt the pressure to define myself by my job or achievements from others. A week before, I ran into someone I used to know from a charity I'd worked for. When she asked me what I was doing for work, I mentioned my degree, but confidently told her, "I'm a writer," as I was working on my first book at the time.

She continued smiling, but some of the genuineness faded from her eyes. "Oh!" she exclaimed. "So you're not looking for a regular job right now?"

I knew she meant well, but as I drove home, I felt the sting of her words. Sitting with them now, I let go of that uncomfortable sensation. Of course, she wouldn't understand. She hadn't undergone the same journey I had. In her mind, career was everything, and the concept of individuality and "doing what you want to do" only applied within an acceptable framework. If she knew my free time mostly consisted of meditation, building Lego sets, and reading whatever brought me joy, she would judge me—harshly.

When I selected the life I did—leaving Todd, finding a future with Bergen—I made a choice that I knew most people would disagree with. Exposing myself to stares and whispers and being the subject of a dinner conversation wasn't my aim, but it came with my divorce and coming out. At the beginning, I tried to control the narrative by posting photos of me on social media in interesting places, surrounded by family. I was all smiles and wide, happy eyes, but sometimes I found myself forcing it just so everyone could see that I hadn't completely blown up my life like they thought—I was *thriving*.

I came to realize that the only person I needed to prove myself to was... myself. The only "likes" I needed were those I gained from my soul. Showing up for myself through self-care was a million times more impactful than any view on my blog. Waiting for other people to comment, "You're amazing!" or "You look so happy!" wouldn't make either of those things a reality.

Deep inside, I still craved validation—that familiar hunger gnawing at my ribs. I wanted someone, anyone, to look at the fragments of my shattered life and tell me they added up to something good, acceptable, meaningful. I'm human; I can't help it. But something shifted when I realized how hollow that validation really was. Once I saw it for what it was, I could finally begin to let it go. I started writing blog posts that I knew might help others struggling through similar darkness, rather than posting carefully curated snapshots designed to make my life appear flawless. My fingers hesitated over the keyboard, trembling slightly as I typed the words "eating disorder" for the first time in a public space.

Opening up about my years with bulimia was excruciating. Each sentence felt like peeling back layers of skin. I gritted my teeth as I described the rituals, the secrets, the shame. When I finally pressed "Publish," my finger hovered for so long that the screen went dark, and I had to wake it again to complete the act. I didn't do it for likes or comments or the performance of vulnerability that had become its own currency. I did it because somewhere, someone needed to hear that they weren't alone. And that was the answer. Helping others—loving them. Knowing my purpose made showing up as myself so easy. Now that I knew how to live it and look for it, I found it everywhere.

Thirty-Six

Joy in Practice, Gratitude in Motion

F OR SO LONG, I thought joy was something that either happened to you or it didn't. I assumed people who radiated happiness must have easier lives, better luck, or lighter burdens.

I didn't realize that joy—like healing, like growth—was something you chose. And that choice, for me, began with gratitude. Not the kind of gratitude that feels performative or forced, but the kind that emerges quietly, through paying attention.

It started with the smallest glimmers. One spring afternoon, driving home along the same route I'd taken for years, something stopped me in my tracks. Lining both sides of the road were cherry blossom trees, their branches heavy with pink and white petals.

Of course, I'd seen them before. They bloomed every year, marking the transition from winter's gray to spring's renewal. But this time was different. This time, I really saw them. The softness of the petals. The way the sunlight filtered through the branches. The fleeting, fragile beauty of it all. And in that moment, I felt something I hadn't felt in a very long time. Not just peace, but a sense of wonder. A sense of aliveness.

That was when I realized joy wasn't something that would arrive fully formed. It wasn't waiting on the other side of healing or at the end of some distant goal. Joy lived in moments. Small, quiet, sacred moments.

As I began to notice more of those moments, I started to see how much beauty had always been around me, waiting patiently for me to pay attention. But noticing wasn't enough. I needed to nurture it. So, Bergen and I started a practice: every night before bed, we would share three things we were grateful for.

Some nights, it was as simple as, The sun felt warm on my face today. Or, We had enough energy to make dinner. Other nights, it was deeper: I stood up for myself today. Or, I felt connected to the boys.

It felt awkward at first, like we were forcing something that didn't want to come naturally. But as the days and weeks passed, I noticed a shift. The more I named what was good, the more I noticed what was good. Gratitude didn't erase the hard things, but it softened them. It offered small glimmers of light I could follow forward.

As our gratitude practice deepened, something else began to change. I started to experience not just fleeting happiness but a deeper sense of aliveness—a vitality I hadn't felt in years.

Joy became less about the big, perfect moments and more about the small, ordinary ones: the first sip of coffee in the morning; Bergen's hand reaching for mine without thinking; the quiet hum of the house settling at night when everyone was safe and asleep. Gratitude had become my invitation to notice the beauty I had overlooked for so long.

As Brené Brown teaches in her TED talk "The Power of Vulnerability," vulnerability is the birthplace of love, belonging, joy, courage, empathy, and creativity. I finally understood that by allowing myself to be vulnerable—to see not just what was good but also what was hard—I had created space for joy to grow.

Practicing gratitude didn't just change how I felt. It changed how I fit.

For years, I had felt disconnected from others. Like I didn't belong anywhere. As a caregiver. As a wife. As a mother navigating my children's complex needs. Even as an advocate, where my purpose often felt isolating. I told myself I didn't mind being alone. And in some ways, I didn't. But deep down, I craved connection. I longed to feel like I belonged—not because I conformed, but because I was accepted for who I really was.

As I leaned into gratitude, I began to see how I was not separate from the world around me. We are all interconnected. My energy flowed into others, and theirs flowed into me. I understood that my intuition wasn't a sign of being "shy" or "too sensitive." It was a gift—a way of tuning into what mattered.

When I embraced my sensitivity and stopped apologizing for needing to protect my energy, my intuition blossomed. My gratitude practice opened that door even wider. I was no longer just surviving. I was living with intention, in flow, grounded in the truth of why I am here.

Life is still hard. That hasn't changed. But I have changed. I now meet each day with the quiet, steady belief that even when joy feels far away, gratitude will always lead me back to it.

Every night, when Bergen and I share our three things, we are not just listing what went well. We are reminding ourselves that joy is not passive. It is a practice. A commitment. A choice. A way of being. And in choosing joy—on purpose—I have found not only a deeper love for others, but for myself.

I am no longer searching for where I belong.

I am already home.

Thirty-Seven

A Letter to the Girl I Used to Be

I F I COULD SIT across from my younger self today—if I could hold her hands and look into her tired eyes—I think I'd start by saying, *You didn't do anything wrong.* You were just trying to survive.

The girl I used to be tried so hard to be perfect. To get it right. To hold everything together with a smile and a schedule and a heart that was always aching beneath the surface. She didn't yet know that no one gets it right. That love doesn't mean self-abandonment. That being "the strong one" isn't a badge you're supposed to wear until you break.

She didn't yet understand that there's no gold medal for pushing yourself past the point of exhaustion. No award for never asking for help. No trophy for pretending you're fine when you're falling apart.

I want to tell her that it's okay to let the mask slip. That softness is not weakness. That the people who truly love you will never ask you to shrink to fit inside a role. I want to hold her close and whisper, *You were always enough.*

I didn't believe that for a long time. Not when I was surrounded by friends and still felt like the odd one out. Not when I was a young mom juggling everything, believing that if I just tried harder, read more, worked more hours, did all the therapies, maybe then I would be worthy. Not even when I was achieving "success"—on paper, in pictures.

But something shifted when I stopped trying to become someone else's idea of a woman, a wife, a mother—and instead, started becoming *me.*

That didn't happen all at once. It happened slowly. It happened in moments that didn't feel like becoming at all. It happened when I admitted that I was scared. It happened when I said no for the first time and meant it. When I let my body rest. When I cried in front of someone I loved and didn't apologize. When I made the hard choice to walk away from a life that looked perfect, but didn't feel like mine.

I look back at that younger version of myself now with tenderness. Not pity. Not regret. But compassion.

She fought for love. She fought for her family. She fought to hold it all together for as long as she could. And then, when she was ready, she chose to let go. Not of her children. Not of her values. But of the lie that said she had to disappear in order to be good.

Now I see her everywhere. She's the woman sitting in her car, taking one more breath before walking into an IEP meeting. She's the mom holding back tears in the grocery store, wondering if anyone sees how hard she's trying. She's the caregiver, the advocate, the quiet soul who's been told her whole life that she's "too sensitive" or "too much" or "not enough." She's the one slowly waking up to the truth that she gets to take up space.

To her, I want to say: Your sensitivity is your superpower. Your voice matters. Your joy matters. You don't have to earn your rest. You don't have to explain your needs. You don't have to wait for permission to live a life that feels like *home.* I know the world taught you to hustle for your worth, to smile through your pain, to push harder, try harder, be more. But I want you to know that becoming isn't about becoming someone *else.* It's about coming home to yourself.

I see that now. And I'm so proud of you.

Epilogue

WE STOOD TOGETHER AT the edge of the water on Orcas Island, the morning sun glinting off the waves. The chapel behind us was quiet now, holding the energy we had brought into it: the vows, the tears, the deep breaths we took when we finally said *I do*.

It wasn't a wedding like the ones I had once imagined. It wasn't perfect in the way the previous version of me would have measured it. But it was real. It was perfect for us. And, it was in the same place I said we would get married on that first weekend away.

Bergen squeezed my hand. I looked at her and smiled—not just because I was happy, but because I felt the weight of the entire journey that had brought me here. The years of self-sacrifice. The motherhood that shaped me and stretched me thin. The marriage I had fought to hold together. The guilt. The unraveling. The letting go. And then—the becoming.

This wasn't the fairytale I once scripted for myself in my twenties. It was something better. Messier. Braver. More honest.

I had regrets. I will always have regrets. I caused pain when I chose to leave my marriage. Real, undeniable pain. For my children. For Todd.

For the life we had built together.

But staying would have destroyed me.

Choosing myself wasn't easy. It wasn't simple. And it didn't mean I stopped loving the people I had built my life with. It meant I finally loved myself enough to stop disappearing.

And I know this: my story of choosing myself might not look like yours. It might look nothing like yours. That's okay. Choosing yourself doesn't always mean leaving. Sometimes it means staying. Sometimes it means speaking up. Sometimes it means risking change in ways no one else can understand.

But whatever it looks like, it's worth the risk. *You* are worth the risk.

As Bergen and I stood at the water's edge, I felt peace, not the absence of struggle, but the true peace that comes from knowing you chose authenticity, even when it was hard.

Becoming wasn't just about choosing myself. It changed how I mothered, too. I began to show up for my boys not as the exhausted, self-sacrificing version of myself I had once been, but as someone who could model resilience, honesty, and self-respect. I set boundaries. I admitted when I didn't have all the answers. I let them see my becoming, not just for myself, but for them.

And as I reclaimed my own voice, my advocacy deepened. I wasn't just fighting for my children's rights—I was fighting for a world where they, too, could live as their fullest, truest selves.

That is the legacy I hope to leave: not perfection, but the courage to live authentically.

I turned toward Bergen. She gave me a quiet, knowing smile. The waves whispered against the shore behind us.

We had arrived at this moment not by chance, but by choice. By the courage to keep becoming, no matter how late it seemed. Because it is never too late.

I came to see that becoming wasn't just an earthly journey. It was a soul remembering. A return to the truest version of myself. As you reach the end of these pages, I hope you'll carry this truth close to your heart: it's never too late.

I know what it feels like to be stuck—to wake up each day feeling like life has hardened around you, like there's no clear way forward. For years, I stood in that place, believing change was either impossible, selfish, or too risky. I thought I had to stay still for the sake of others. But the truth is, even when we feel frozen, *small steps are always possible.* And those small steps—tiny, quiet choices—are where everything begins.

You don't have to upend your life overnight—or at all. You don't have to have all the answers. You only have to begin. Listen to the gentle nudge of your intuition—we all have it. Seek out small joys. Speak your truth in little ways. Let yourself hope again.

Your path will be your own. And along the way, you may be surprised by what you discover—about courage, about love, about the quiet, unstoppable power of becoming who you were always meant to be.

The next chapter of your story is waiting. I can't wait to see what you create.

Acknowledgments

To my sons—you are, and always will be, my greatest teachers. You have challenged me, inspired me, and given my life meaning in ways words can never fully capture. Everything I have become I owe in part to you. I love you with all my heart and being your mom is my greatest joy.

To Bergen—your patience, kindness, and belief in my growth helped me find the courage to rewrite my life. You never asked me to change. You simply witnessed my becoming and stood beside me, offering steady love without conditions. I am grateful for the home we have built together. Thank you for walking beside me, not just through the joyful moments, but through every uncertain step that brought us here.

To my daughters—thank you for welcoming me into your lives with such warmth and grace. Being part of your world has brought me unexpected joy and a deeper sense of family than I ever imagined.

To Mom—thank you for loving me exactly as I am and for always believing in who I could become. Your unwavering support has meant everything to me.

Companion Journal: A Guide for Your Own Becoming

By Lanya Lynn Elsa

A Note to the Reader

This guide is for anyone who has ever asked: "Is it too late to choose myself?"

Whether you're navigating grief, identity, parenting, love, or a complete reinvention of your life, this is your space to pause, reflect, and breathe. You don't need to have all the answers. Just an open heart and the courage to ask the questions.

Part I: Foundations – Early Lessons on Loneliness, Desire, and Belonging

"Before I could come home to myself, I had to understand the girl who got lost trying to belong."

Journal Prompts:

- When was the first time you remember dimming your light to fit in?

- What messages about "being good" did you internalize growing up?

- How did early friendships and romantic relationships shape the way you see yourself today?

- Who were you before the world told you who to be?

- In what ways have you abandoned or protected your inner child?

Part II: The Identities That Shaped Me

"It wasn't a breakdown—it was a remembering."

Journal Prompts:

- What identities have you carried that once served you, but now feel heavy?

- Have you ever felt like the only one in the room who truly understood your child's needs?

- What did you sacrifice to hold it all together? What would it mean to put it down?

- In what ways have you shown up for others even when your own tank was empty?

- What does it look like for you to become, not just survive?

Part III: Awakening – Coming Home to Myself

"This wasn't about logic anymore. This was about healing."

Journal Prompts:

- What does your intuition sound like? Do you trust it?

- What healing modalities have supported your journey? (Reiki, energy work, therapy, writing, etc.)

- What part of yourself are you still learning to love?

- Have you ever chosen joy even when it felt selfish or scary?

- What truth have you been afraid to speak aloud?

Final Reflection: Writing Your Own Becoming

- Who are you now that you weren't before?

- What are you ready to release?

- What legacy do you want to leave—not in perfection, but in truth?

- Write a letter to your past self, thanking them for surviving.

- Write a letter to your future self, promising them you won't abandon them again.

About the Author

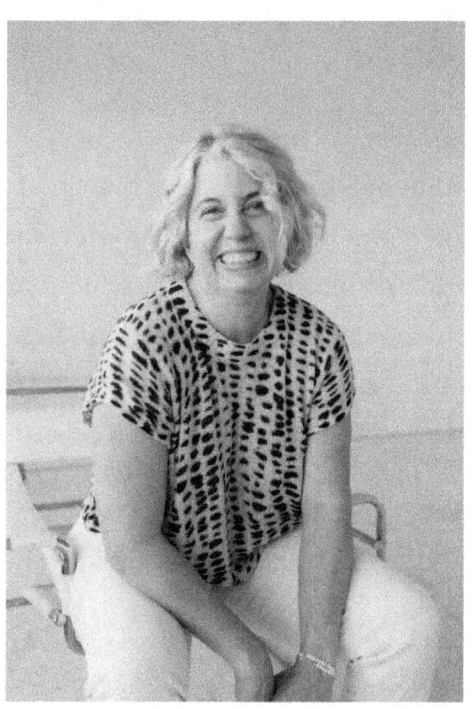

Lanya Lynn Elsa, PhD (formerly Lanya McKittrick), is a mother, advocate, researcher, and a woman who has found strength through self-reflection, intuition, and healing. She is the proud mom of four sons and two stepdaughters, including two sons who are deafblind due to Usher syndrome—a rare genetic condition that reshaped her world and gave rise to a lifelong calling.

Through years of navigating complex systems, Lanya became a trusted advocate—not just for her own children, but for families like hers across the country. That work eventually led her to earn a doctorate in Special Education and build a career grounded in lived experience.

But it was the personal unraveling—after heartbreak, identity shifts, and the quiet ache of putting herself last for too long—that became her most sacred work. Becoming the Woman I Needed tells that story: one of motherhood, love, and the long, beautiful process of coming home to yourself.

She is also the author of Silence and Light, a memoir about parenting through uncertainty and building a life around what matters most. Lanya remains deeply connected to the deafblind community through her research, writing, and family advocacy. She speaks and teaches nationally on special education, disability rights, and the power of lived experience to drive both systemic change and collective healing.

She lives in the Pacific Northwest with her wife and children, where she continues to write, heal, and walk alongside others on their own journey of becoming.

Learn more at www.lanyaelsa.com

www.ingramcontent.com/pod-product-compliance
Lightning Source LLC
Chambersburg PA
CBHW060131130626
46556CB00006B/2313